BROKEN HOPE RESTORED

SEVEN TRUE STORIES OF TRANSFORMED LIVES
IN CHARLOTTE, MICHIGAN

This book was written for the express purpose of conveying the love and mercy of Jesus Christ. The statements in this book are substantially true; however, names and minor details have been changed to protect people and situations from accusation or incrimination.

All Scripture quotations, unless otherwise noted, are taken from the New International Version Copyright 1973, 1984, 1987 by International Bible Society.

Published by GCP. V1.1

Printed in the United States of America

TABLE OF CONTENTS

DEDICATION

To those who long for hope and healing,
we hope you find both within these pages.

ACKNOWLEDGEMENTS

I would like to thank Randy Royston for his vision for this book and Carol Kelley for her hard work in making it a reality. To those who shared their personal stories, thank you for your boldness and vulnerability.

This book would not have been published without the amazing efforts of our project manager and editor, Hayley Pandolph. Her untiring resolve pushed this project forward and turned it into a stunning victory. Thank you for your great fortitude and diligence. Deep thanks to our incredible editor in chief, Michelle Cuthrell, and executive editor, Jen Genovesi, for all the amazing work they do. I would also like to thank our invaluable proofreader, Melody Davis, for the focus and energy she puts into perfecting our words.

Lastly, I want to extend our gratitude to the creative and very talented Ariana Randle, who designed the beautiful cover for *Broken Hope Restored: Seven True Stories of Transformed Lives in Charlotte, Michigan.*

Daren Lindley
President and CEO
Good Catch Publishing

The book you are about to read
is a compilation of authentic life stories.
The facts are true, and the events are real.
These storytellers have dealt with crisis, tragedy, abuse
and neglect and have shared their most private moments,
mess-ups and hang-ups in order for others to learn and
grow from them. In order to protect the identities of those
involved in their pasts, the names and details of some
storytellers have been withheld or changed.

INTRODUCTION

Nobody aspires to become a murderer, an addict or a victim of abuse. We don't expect our marriages to end. We don't imagine our children will die. But these things happen. Every day. To people all around us.

Broken hopes, dreams and promises can be devastating. The stories you are about to read offer remarkable accounts of real people right here in Charlotte, Michigan, who experienced heartache, pain and loss — and then overcame setbacks and hardships to live with real meaning, purpose and joy.

Learn from these amazing people the secrets that brought about their breakthroughs. Learn how they rediscovered hope and transformed their lives. Be inspired that you, too, can find HOPE for tomorrow!

SENTENCED TO LIFE
THE STORY OF HARLEY
WRITTEN BY KEVIN KREBS

The door slammed shut. It always made an unsettling sound, an unmistakable clang, when they closed that steel and iron door — vertical bars interlaced with horizontal supports and painted black. Hundreds of hands had grasped the chipped paint and rusted metal of those bars before me. Like me, waiting, hoping for release.

The door clicked, securing the lock to my concrete tomb in the Michigan State Prison. Voices echoed from the hundreds of identical cells around me in all directions, above and below. I wondered what my life would be like on this side of the bars. What irony, going from a brief career as a corrections officer to a life behind these bars.

This stretch would be different than my prior prison terms and jail sentences. In those, hope remained a possibility, either waiting for my release date or the next parole hearing. This time, the doors leading out of the prison gate would not be opened. I was a lifer.

I rubbed my chin, feeling the long strands of my beard. *It's their fault,* I thought, *not mine. I'm in control. I'm in charge of my life. I did nothing wrong.* I remembered my father. I could see his face clearly, even though it had been 11 years since he'd walked the earth. *It's his fault!* My mind screamed those words.

"Hey, Harley, what're you in for?" The words escaped from an unseen soul located in the cell next to mine. They were formed by a gravelly voice aged by years of incarceration.

"Partner," I said, low laugh following, "I'm innocent."

"Aren't we all," came the reply, followed by silence.

I thought back to the courtroom nearly two years earlier where I pled guilty to the murder of what I regarded as two pieces of human garbage who got what they deserved. Back to the sound of the judge's voice pronouncing my sentence — life without parole. And then back even earlier, to a life filled with everything a 30-year-old guy would want or desire.

అఆఅ

That summer in Lansing, Michigan, sweltered. It was only 82 degrees, but as I worked in my body shop, I felt like I was in the jungles back in Vietnam. As I worked, I glanced out the door of the building at a bevy of cars parked in the back lot of my business. Included was my shiny Corvette, parked next to my Harley Davidson Sportster. Back at home were my weekend drives, expensive antique cars and classic vehicles that impressed everyone.

My home was the party house on weekends for friends wanting a safe place to have fun. The alcohol always flowed, and the girls always arrived, though they were not part of my life — I was never a part of that equation. I found my comfort each morning in a quart of Jack Daniels to get my day rolling.

Lori arrived at the house one hot June day. I was feeling pretty cheerful after having ingested a number of beers, losing count after the fifth. As I looked at her face, young and pretty, I could not ignore the ugly bruises, the result of what I guessed was a pretty good beating.

"Let me ask you a question. It's none of my business, but what are you into, masochism or something?" I held a can of Budweiser steadily in my hand.

Lori looked down, refusing eye contact. "No," came the soft reply, "I've got a boyfriend who likes to beat me up."

I set the can down on the table in front of me, leaning toward her for emphasis. "Call the cops on him."

"I can't. If I call the cops, they'll call my parents, and they're going to make me come home, and I don't want to go home."

I retrieved the can of Bud from the table, took a long drink before responding. "That's a helluva price to pay for your freedom."

Over the next two months, Lori frequently came to the house, looking for the kind of welcome she found nowhere else. Only she couldn't hide the constant bruises on her face.

One night while I was enjoying a drink, Lori arrived at the house, her face beaten once again. I had seen enough. I pointed to the phone on the nearby table, and her eyes followed my finger.

"Get this guy on the phone."

Lori dialed. After a brief silence a conversation ensued. Or maybe an argument. She pleaded with him, but it was obvious it was not working. Taking the phone from her trembling hand, it was my turn.

"The lady just told you she can't deal with it," I growled into the phone.

"Wait a minute, man. Who are you?" came the response.

"Why, I'm a little nobody."

The voice on the phone issued an empty threat and expressed his strong dislike for me.

"I know exactly who you are. The lady said she can't deal with it. Do it again. If you don't like me now, then you'll like me even less." I slammed the phone down. If I had only known at the time the pain Lori was really feeling.

In late September, at 10 a.m., I had begun my ritual of Jack Daniels and Budweiser and was well into it when Lori arrived at the house. When I opened the door, I saw her once-beautiful face covered in black and blue. Her fine features were undistinguishable beneath her injuries.

"Tonight, Lori, you'll have a celebration instead of a party, 'cause it won't happen again." My words faded as I went to my bedroom and walked to the unmade bed. Reaching my hand under the pillow, my fingers felt the cold steel of a .38 Special. Turning, I placed the gun in my waistband and smiled. I was a god, and the power of life and death was in my hand.

I first drove myself to the home I knew Lori's boyfriend occupied. Finding no one home, I drove the short distance to where he worked at a nearby gas station. I got a Coke and spent the next 15 minutes looking around until I saw my target, all 6 feet, 2 inches of him, standing a few feet away.

I forced a smile. "Is your name Edward?"

He eyed me suspiciously. "Yes, it is. Why?"

"Do you know Lori?"

His demeanor suddenly changed, eyes narrowing, light wrinkles appearing on his 21-year-old face. "So what if I do?"

I equaled his gaze. "I'm that little nobody."

The words barely escaped my mouth when Edward put his arms out and began walking toward me. "Who the h— " he shouted as he fell to the ground.

I didn't notice the explosion in my hand as the .38 round left the chamber. I didn't even realize the method of Edward's execution until it was over. From 8 feet away, a friend of Edward's who had been listening to the conversation realized what had happened and wanted to be a hero. He fell down, too.

I returned home, and Lori called me on the phone, panicked. By then the media frenzy over the double murder had spread, and she knew what I'd done. I assured her she would not be implicated.

"Everything I've done, I just did on my own," I said to her. "What I did, I did."

An hour after the call, a friend of my wife called and

told me Edward got what he deserved. "He needed killing a long time ago," she said and went on to tell me how Edward would beat Lori up and force her to have sex with different men, filming the encounters and selling the movies.

I was arrested and sentenced to spend the rest of my natural life behind bars, a place I had known all too well, my idyllic life gone, freedom removed from my sight. *It wasn't my fault,* I thought. *It was his fault. Edward is responsible.* For a moment, I thought of my father. *And his.*

Looking into the mirror on my cell wall one day, I combed my graying hair. My shirtless chest was darkened by tattoos, drawing on memories from all over the world. I stopped combing as a thought flashed in my head.

Supposin' it ain't everybody else? Supposin' it's you?

૰૰૰

We were two miles up the holler, the base of the valley between very tall hills traversing some seven miles off the main road. I was a small boy and very aware of it. My first years of life were harsh, though many people did not know the life of luxury growing up in the hills of West Virginia in 1948.

My father was married to my mother. He had stolen her from her previous husband. She abandoned all but one of her nine boys and six girls, leaving them to her surprised husband so she could be with my father, bringing one daughter to live with us in a small ramshackle two-bedroom house. Living with no running water, no electricity or gas, I remember more than my fair share of freezing nights running to the outhouse.

While my father worked a meager existence in a sawmill and as a carpenter, my mother spent her days cooking on a wood-burning stove and using coal in a potbellied stove strategically placed in our living room to keep us warm.

I would run off to school in one of my allotted two pairs of pants and two shirts, taking great care not to tear or damage the garments, which had to last me for the entire school year. Returning home from school one day, walking casually and busting dirt clods I found along the road with the heels of my feet, I noticed one of the hogs was missing from the pen. That night we enjoyed a meal, thanks to the missing swine.

When Dad was not working, he was salting and smoking meat rendered from the hogs and other livestock sharing the space we called home. I spent my evenings in the summertime tending to a garden and a 2-acre plot of strawberries on a nearby hillside.

On many Saturday afternoons, we would embark on a journey to town. My sister and I would see the latest movie, usually my favorite, a movie featuring cowboys. I would mimic what I saw, the cowboy with his shiny gun and tall hat, an American icon.

Nosing around in my parents' room, I found a treasure stashed in a top dresser drawer under my father's clothes. I examined the compact gun and how it fit in my hand, the brown handle perfectly matching the curves and ridges in my hand. I spun the black barrel of the .38 Smith & Wesson and saw a cylinder waiting to be fed five bullets.

From the front porch of my house, I spent hours practicing firing the gun, feeling the power I held in my hands, the power of life and death. I was 9.

In 1953, my father left my mother, taking me with him. The two of us spent the next years traveling across the country, my father building houses in new development after new development. I soon learned the pleasures and curses of drinking.

By the age of 12, I was living in a trailer park with my father in the town of Amarillo, Texas. The 16-foot trailer was parked next to the manager's office. One day in October, I found myself not interested in attending school and, with a friend two years my senior, decided to take a day off.

We entered the trailer, opening the refrigerator to look for food when Gary saw it, a half-gallon of Mogen David wine resting on a shelf. On the side of the bottle, my father marked how much remained after he drank his obligatory 8 ounces with dinner. "I need to keep my blood thin," my father would say before issuing a stern warning. "Son, if you ever *touch* this bottle, you'll get a whippin' like you've never seen." I remembered the beatings he gave me when I was younger. I believed him.

Gary pulled the wine out of the refrigerator and opened the cap.

"Oh, no, no, no, no," I said, "my dad will beat me to death."

Gary smirked at me. "You can't stop me because you can't whip me."

I walked quickly to the back of the trailer and, looking in my father's room, saw what I needed. Almost as quickly, I returned to the kitchen. Gary still held the bottle.

"Put that bottle of wine down because I'm not going to take a beatin' over you."

Gary stood motionless at first, not reacting to the .22 rifle pointed directly at him. He then took a step toward me, and I pulled the trigger. I expected to hear an empty click, assuming my father stored the gun unloaded.

A loud pop broke the silence, and Gary fell to the ground.

After a phone call from the trailer park manager, my father returned home. Gary was more fortunate than I was going to be at the hands of my father. The bullet had entered his body just above his belt, passed through him, through our couch, out the side of the trailer and into the manager's office where it lodged in a steel desk. Gary suffered no major damage.

After being remanded to adult court, I was tried for assault with a deadly weapon and sentenced to 18 months in prison where, at 4 feet, 8 inches, I was introduced to the Texas state prison system.

As they opened the door into the prison's housing unit, I was met with the stench of 500 men who hadn't showered in days. Walking to my cell, I looked in the faces of the incarcerated men who watched me. Some whistled catcalls my way, while others viewed me as a would-be son.

Overcome with fear, I realized the next year and a half of my life would be spent with men a least a foot taller and 100 pounds heavier than me. Those seemed like insurmountable odds.

I wandered around inside the housing unit and was approached by a man who glanced from side to side. He reached out his hand in what looked like a gesture of friendship. As my hand reached to meet his, I felt him place a cold steel object in my palm.

"Here, you're gonna need this," he said as he continued walking.

I hid the knife in my solitary cell and spent the first few nights sleeping with my back against the wall, worrying who might reach through the cell bars or who might pick open the lock to my cell door and pay me a visit.

I knew from that day forward, I'd have to fight for my life. The guards always seemed to look away, showing no concern for the violence and crimes committed inside the prison by one prisoner against another.

Eventually, I made a device a man showed me. He called it a stinger. After stealing two spoons from the cafeteria and electrical tape and wires from another part of the prison, I flattened out the spoons and taped a wire to each one. I pushed the wires into an electrical outlet in my cell and dropped the spoons below the outlet into a small wastebasket filled with water.

One night, the sound of metal against metal from the lock in my cell door woke me. In the dim light, I could see the door swing open, and in walked a man with intentions I didn't wait to find out. I grasped the water-filled wastebasket and flung the liquid at the man's face.

His screams from the scalding water could be heard throughout the prison.

かかか

"I want you to call me Mom." Her voice told me this woman from North Carolina was not as sweet as she looked.

I shook my head no. She was not my mother, and she would not be my mother.

My relationship with my father's latest wife was not a pleasant one. Not seeing eye-to-eye on anything with my mother, my father tried to convince me my mother was unworthy to be called Mom, and this woman would take her place.

I disagreed.

My father arranged for my early release from the prison in Amarillo. Promising the judge we would never return to Texas, I was granted the early reprise, and we immediately moved to Maryland.

My stepmother brought me new clothes every weekend. I remember a white pair of Levi's and a black shirt she gave me and how cool I looked. After giving me the clothes, she walked down the hall to my father's room. She shut the door.

I listened carefully to her words. "I gave that little bastard of yours some more clothes."

Rage filled me as I returned to my room and found all the clothes she'd ever given me and threw them on my bed. I wrapped them up in a bedspread and found the only clothing I had that she was not responsible for — cutoff jeans and a T-shirt. I put them on, along with a ragged pair of Converse tennis shoes.

Walking down the hall to my father's room, I kicked the door open and threw the bedspread with the wrapped clothing on their bed.

"Let me tell you something, you're not my mother, you'll never be my mother, and let me tell you something else, witch — I am not for sale!"

Leaving the house, I walked down the street. Soon I heard a distinctive rattle, and I knew it was my father in his '56 Chevy. Pulling up beside me, he stopped the car, and I stopped walking.

"Get in the car," he said.

Opening the door, I slid into the seat next to my father. I refused to look at him.

"Where you going?" he asked.

"I don't know."

"When you coming back?" He turned toward me.

I looked at him. "I'm not."

"How are you gonna live?"

"I don't know," I answered quietly.

"You got a job?"

I looked at the floor of the car. "No."

"I'm taking you home." My father turned, shifting the car into drive and turning it around toward home.

I glared at him, anger welling from deep inside. "Are you ready to chain me to the bed?"

Pulling off to the side of the road, he stopped the car. "What did you say?"

"Are you ready to chain me to the bed?"

"No, why?"

I refused to break eye contact. "Because the second you leave that driveway, I'm right behind you."

My father turned away. He reached into his back pocket, pulling out his wallet. He handed me a familiar green piece of paper. I rubbed the $20 bill in my fingers, examining the portrait of Andrew Jackson.

"Keep in touch," he said.

The air was cold, seeping deep into my bones. My first winter as a 13-year-old was spent sleeping in the front of an abandoned and junked 1956 Ford Crown Victoria. But I felt free. Shivering, I looked at all the possessions I had in life arranged on the seat of that car. A mirror, a candle, a sleeping bag and, the most important possession of all, a .38 Smith & Wesson revolver.

≈≈≈

"You know, Harley," the prison guard said. "I've never seen anything like this. You have gone from a young man to an old man after only nine months in this place."

I adjusted my reading glasses, looked up from my book and through the bars at the officer standing on the catwalk outside my cell. I realized he was right. In a short period of time since being sentenced to life, I had aged rapidly.

My once-full head of brown hair had turned gray and was rapidly falling out. I was no longer the young man who'd entered the Michigan State Prison at age 34.

Time passed, and I learned quickly how to survive, using the same tools I had used on the outside, now on the inside. Knives, fists, whatever I had available, they were all part of my existence.

As a decade of my sentence went by, I realized I could never get along with anybody and found myself always at odds with everybody, fellow inmates, guards and the system. Then I remembered that day I looked into the mirror.

Supposin' it ain't everybody else? Supposin' it's you?

As the years passed, I realized after much internal soul searching, it really was me, and I understood why nobody liked me. I was the source of the problem, not everybody else. I made myself a deal. I was going to get out of bed every morning with only one intent in mind — not to harm anybody, including myself.

It was 2007 when I first heard the words. "It's called ex post facto," said the man in the cell next to me.

It was 25 years into my life sentence, and a fellow prisoner had filed a lawsuit on behalf of all the lifers incarcerated in the Michigan State Prison.

"Look at it this way," he said. "If you are charged with a crime today and say you have a five-year maximum sentence and then the law is changed to a seven-year sentence, the harsher sentence cannot be applied to you since it is greater than the punishment you started with."

"Okay," I said, nodding.

"Us lifers, we went from sentence reviews every two years to reviews every five years," he said. He continued as he figured the math, "This means your eligibility for parole went from 10 years to 30 years. That means the sentences are harsher. And they can't do that."

It sounded like a good idea to me. He filed his lawsuit on behalf of 1,000 lifers. Unfortunately, the courts didn't agree, and he lost the suit, but not before a decision was made that ended in the parole of 199 of those 1,000 prisoners serving life sentences.

I was included in the group of prisoners slated for release. In a meeting with a counselor preparing me for my entrance back into the world outside of the prison walls, he made a suggestion.

"I think you should try Alcoholics Anonymous."

I looked at him strangely. "Have you lost your mind?"

He was surprised at my attitude. "Why would you say that?"

"Because for 30 years, every day when I opened my eyes and realized where I was at, I understood just exactly what the bottle does for me, partner. I spent the last 30 years of my life over a bottle of booze."

Finally, on October 17, 2012, I made parole.

❧ ❧ ❧

To call it an apartment was an insult. It was more of a small room inside a crowded and dilapidated building. I was told furniture was not supplied, and I needed to be glad with what I had. What I had was a nasty old mattress thrown on a soiled floor.

I looked around and took stock of what possessions I had and, more obviously, what I didn't have. Food.

A man from housing services was kind enough to help me, and I found a small food bank. At the food bank, I met Phil, a man who seemed to take an interest in me, for what reason I didn't know. He gave me a small basket of food, and I left to return to my new home.

I realized after entering the apartment with the food, I had nothing to cook the food in. No pots, no stove, no microwave. Just the food. Returning to the food bank, I once again saw Phil happily handing out baskets to other downtrodden souls.

I got his attention. "Just tell me what the hell I'm supposed to do here," I said, "if they're not going to give me nothing. The state has yet to give me one single red cent when I came out of prison."

Still smiling, Phil asked, "Well, what do you need?"

"I've got a whole list as long as your arm of things that I need."

"What are you doing this afternoon?" Phil asked.

I thought for a moment. "Well, my calendar's full, but I can probably fit you in." I smirked.

That afternoon, Phil took me to Walmart and in a short period of time we were at the checkout with a full shopping cart. When the clerk rang up the tally, I saw $150. We left the store, and I wondered who this man was and why he cared about me. For the first time in my life, someone treated me like I was a human being.

Phil saw the expression on my face. "Look here, I want you to know something. I'm not an easy mark. God just told me that you were worthy of being helped."

I didn't know how to answer. I stared at him.

Phil paused. "I'd like you to go to church with me."

"No, no, no, we can't do that, dude," I told him. "We can do a lot of things, but we can't go to church." I remembered the last time I tried to set foot in a church many years before at my sister-in-law's wedding. It was a hot day, and the church was cool, but every time I stepped inside the building, the temperature mysteriously rose.

Phil sensed my apprehension. "Why not? Give me a good reason."

I couldn't find one.

࿇࿇࿇

"This is the perfect church for imperfect people," Pastor Randy announced from his position on a small stage covered in brown carpet three steps up from the main floor. Behind him, a wooden pulpit stood unused, and a large wooden cross hung on the wall.

I nodded from my seat inside New Hope Community Church.

Pastor Randy continued. "God can make a difference in your life. The people in this building feed off of the word of God. Understand, we are imperfect people, and God is the God of all people."

Just two weeks after Phil first invited me to his church, I found myself sitting in a building I thought I would never enter. During the service, I felt a feeling of peace and tranquility, something I never remember having before.

He brought you here, Harley, showing you the pits of hell to show you the other side, giving you the opportunity to just look, I thought to myself.

Do you want this or what you were doing? asked a voice I thought I heard beside me, where no one sat.

I shook my head no and felt the death of the old man I used to be and the birth of a new soul. I knew in that moment the old guy was dead, his ways were dead, as was the way he'd thought about things.

After the service, I spoke with Pastor Randy. He shook my hand firmly. I reciprocated. "I think you should know I've done the last 30 years in prison for a double shooting."

Pastor Randy smiled, refusing to let go of my hand.

"If you want me to leave the premises, I will honor that request."

"No — please stay. You're an answered prayer for coming here." He smiled at me.

Over time, it was a gradual progression to fully accepting Christ in my life. The more I attended church, the more I fit in and felt like God directed me to tell anybody who was willing to listen about my history and how God changed me. I felt like his hand was on my shoulder.

☙☙☙

The work on the apartment was finished. The tenant, being very gracious, invited me to have a cold drink with him. Thankfully, he did not offer alcohol. This didn't happen all the time as I completed my job — maintenance work on apartments my employer managed. Maybe it was the connection. He had just been released from prison.

My employer frequently rented to men coming out of prison. I found that my work in those apartments put me in a position to talk to men who listened to me.

"You know," I said between sips of the cold iced tea, "you can live your life any way you want, but for 60 years, I've done exactly that."

The man nodded. His eyes told me he understood.

"I've lived my life according to my rules. Well, I ended up just where you did, spending years doing it my way."

"But we're both out now."

"Yes." I paused for effect. "But for how long? How long until, living by your own rules, you fall back into the same trap and end up back where you came from? Of all the lifers I was released with, I'm the only one still free, partner. The rest are all back in."

He looked at the floor, contemplating something deep.

"I know you're not religious, but let me tell you what God has done for me. God has had mercy on my soul and has shown me there was a chance at real life if I just trusted in him."

He looked back at me. I could see agreement in his eyes.

I told him at length where I had come from, where I had been and the path I walked that led me to spend the better years of my life in prison. I told him in detail what God had done for me.

Setting my drink down, I knew it was time to leave. He remained in his chair, deep in thought. I invited him to go with me to church the following week.

❧ ❧ ❧

"You ought to write a book. Tell your story," Phil said to me.

"A book?" I asked.

"Get the story out, the transformation. Tell the message God wants you to get out."

We neared the entrance to New Hope Community Church, and I stopped walking.

"I know the message, Phil. I had wandered through life for 35 to 40 years, knowing I was on a fast track to hell. I was destined to die in prison."

"That's my point, Harley, write your story."

"I don't think I should be diggin' up bones."

Phil looked puzzled. "Bones?"

The song from Randy Travis played in my head.

I'm diggin' up bones, I'm diggin' up bones
Exhuming things that's better left alone.

"I think at this time, I just need to get the word out. Tell whoever will listen my story. Sometimes there are things that need to be left alone." I smiled and entered the church.

Standing in the foyer, I looked around at the people who, like me, have found this church, noticing all the imperfect people standing around me, in shorts and flip-flops, down-to-earth people who know in their life there have been challenges and they can rise up to meet them.

Patting me on the back, one man said to me, "Harley, I can't believe you were in prison — you're not that type of guy. You're a wonderful guy, a man with compassion with a heart who cares."

I nodded, not finding the words to respond. These were words I was not used to hearing. Standing behind me as I entered the church was Phil, a man who took my hand in his and guided me in the right direction. With his guidance, I soon found my true Savior.

Anytime I think about God, a feeling comes over me, not necessarily of tranquility, not even peace. I have a hard time believing this all happened because of the grace of God. It's hard to believe that I am now someone respected in the community.

When I was recently asked about forgiveness, I said, "I

would not want to die tomorrow because I have so many things I would like to make amends for. So many people go through life just existing, not going forward and not going backward. God has shown me there is a world and a hereafter and there is a certain way you need to live. If you're willing to accept this, this can be your reward now and forever."

My other reward was meeting Elizabeth, a Christian woman with a strong faith, morals and principles. She is one in a million, second only to God in my life. I didn't think I'd ever find someone of her caliber, but I did. We married, and I've never been happier in my life.

On a daily basis, my routine requires me to pass the spot where I was arrested decades ago. It reminds me of my wandering in this life, knowing that I was on a fast track for hell and knowing now I have taken a different path toward God.

SNATCHED
THE STORY OF BECKY
WRITTEN BY SARAH REYNOLDS

I could feel their eyes on me. As my cousin Abby and I went from one area of the park to another, four teenagers and one man off in the distance slowly migrated in our direction, watching our every move. If we moved from the merry-go-round to the swings, they moved toward the swings. If we moved from the swings to the monkey bars, they moved to the monkey bars.

"I'm scared, Abby," I whispered. "They're watching us."

"Let's run," Abby suggested, also scared.

I wasn't familiar with the park because I was just visiting Abby and her family for a week. I didn't live in that city and had never been to that park before that day, when we rode our bikes there together.

We ran and hid inside a bathroom. We each stood on a toilet so our feet wouldn't show, then we locked the bathroom stall doors.

"Shhh," I whispered. "They're outside." I could hear them running about outside the bathroom and knew they were looking for us.

My heart raced, and my whole body shook. Every part of me filled with fear. We stood still and waited for the sound of their footsteps outside the door to fade in the distance.

"I think they're gone," Abby said quietly.

I stepped down from the toilet, unlatched the door and tiptoed out of the stall, then moved cautiously beyond the cement walls enclosing the bathroom area only to come face-to-face with the man. I instantly filled with fear again, adrenaline pounding throughout my body, as he scooped me up and ran off with me. They didn't take Abby — only me.

అ౦ అ౦ అ౦

As a child, I never told anyone. Not Abby. Not my uncle Steve. Not my parents. Nobody.

I never discussed what happened at the playground. I never told what happened afterward.

I was 8 years old when I visited Abby's family.

For years and years, I had nightmares. Fears I couldn't explain.

The dark.

Big Victorian houses.

Certain number sequences.

Often, I had dreams of being followed or chased. Even as an adult, if I drove at night and a car followed me for any distance, I'd panic.

Another recurring dream hounded me. I was running through grass. I could see it flowing under my feet as I ran. My concentration in the dream was always on the grass and running as fast as I could. At times, the dream broadened to include a park I couldn't identify.

As a child, I also drew the same picture. I'd be doodling to pass the time. It was always the same: A big house with many rooms, a fence around it and a swing set. Always a swing set.

Even when I played in the snow, I'd make a trail in the snow in the shape of a big house with lots of square rooms. Much like the "fox and hound" game kids play in the snow, I made pictures of the big houses in my mind and would walk through the rooms.

෨෨෨

When I was in my 30s, my husband and I moved with our children into the house I grew up in. That's when my memory flashes began.

෨෨෨

"If you don't keep your mouth shut, this is what's going to happen to you," one of the men told me as he lifted a white sheet to reveal a dead body.

I stood in the backyard of a large house where several bodies lay covered in white sheets. So crippled with fear, I could barely walk. They dragged me inside, holding tightly to my arms. I was too terrified to resist.

Inside, it was dark, but I saw people of all ages — men and women, as well as children. Every time they showed me something terrifying, like one of them skinning a cat alive, they warned, "This is what will happen to you if you tell anyone." They weren't physically hurting me, but they were putting fear in me beyond anything my mind could process.

I spent several hours there that night, then when they were certain I was so terrified I wouldn't tell anyone where they'd taken me and what they'd shown me, they took me back to Abby's parents' house and dropped me off in the front yard of their duplex.

That night, as I huddled in fear, no one asked where I'd been. Abby was tucked in asleep, so I went to bed and covered my face and body with the blankets, still shaking with fear.

❧❧❧

The next night, someone came and took me from Abby's house when everyone else was asleep. I didn't scream or fight them because I knew what they'd do to me if I did. When I arrived at the large house again, I was surrounded by many of the same disturbing people from the night before. The people who lived in the neighboring duplex to Uncle Steve's home were a few of the faces I saw. By sunrise, I was tired and growing even more uncertain of my fate.

"What's your name?" a woman in charge asked me.

"Becky," I answered. She slapped me across my face. I didn't understand why she was so angry with me, but I didn't question her as she dragged me outside and threw me into a dirt hole in the ground. I sat there for hours, not knowing if anyone was going to come get me or if I would be left there all night. I feared the worst and thought maybe I would be left there to die. By now, the sun was shining over the hole, and I was feeling the summer's heat on my body. I was thirsty and hungry and trying to pass the time as each hour wore on. I scribbled in the cold dirt with my fingernails, drawing pictures, then wiping them away to start over again — anything to keep my mind occupied.

As the sun began to set, the same woman came back to get me from the hole, and I was taken to my uncle's for the night.

ক্কক্কক্ক

The next day, I was taken again without force. I knew I had to go with the people who came for me each day — there was never a struggle to take me. I was always made accessible to them through the routines of Abby's home.

"What's your name?" the woman asked me again.

"Becky," I answered. I wasn't trying to be coy or give her reason to toss me in the hole again. I just didn't know what answer she was looking for me to give.

She tossed me in the hole. This time, after several hours of being in the hole, when I was let out and she asked me my name again, I made one up.

"My name is Tammy," I answered, and she seemed pleased with it. She didn't care what I called myself, as long as I knew I was no longer myself and my name was no longer Becky.

❧❧❧

Night after night, throughout the entire week I visited my uncle, I was taken to the large house with the dead bodies and the dirt hole in the backyard. I never told anyone, including my parents, because I was told over and over by the people who took me that they'd kill my family and me if I told anyone.

By the end of it, I had a new name and was assigned a baby to take care of and an older woman was put in charge of me. It was her job to encourage me to do what I was told to avoid being hurt. The baby was to keep me in line.

"From now on, you do what we say, or we'll kill your baby," they warned. "No matter where you are, you do what we tell you or you'll both die."

Being a child myself, I was tortured by the idea that these people would harm a baby to punish me. I was responsible for the baby. By the time I went back home, I knew I couldn't tell anyone and couldn't turn away from what was happening to me.

❧❧❧

In case I started to get the courage up to share with anyone what had happened, one of the people from the house would come lurking, instilling more fear in me. It was common for them to be at the grocery store or near my school after I went home, showing up with the baby as it grew into a toddler and a young child, reminding me to keep my mouth shut. Uncle Steve and Abby lived several hours from my home, but the people still showed up just to make sure I was paying attention. The entire purpose of the abduction was to prime me for what was to come.

రావించి

Over the years, I wouldn't necessarily know why, but something simple would trigger fear in me. A piece of mail. A phone call.

Later, only one explanation made sense to me: I'd been programmed to suppress my memories until the moment the cult wanted to send me a reminder of what I'd seen and what they would do to me if I told anyone.

"Meet us in Atlanta, Georgia," a voice on the phone *might say, giving me instructions about when and where I was supposed to go. It was always a big Victorian house with great rooms and huge grounds. All the "guests" dressed in sophisticated attire. All ritualistic meetings or ceremonies occurred in the home, outside on the grounds or in various outbuildings.*

By the time I was 18, I was free to manage my own life and drive to wherever they asked me to go. When I started to consciously recall and understand what had happened, I realized that from the time they first took me, they must have been preparing me for when I was old enough to fully participate in the cult, whether I wanted to be part of it or not.

I didn't feel I had a choice and was still trying to protect the baby, who was now a young child, as well as my own family, as the threats continued regularly.

It happened again and again. I would be called upon to meet them in various places, sometimes being shown more things to frighten me, other times just to get in my head with repeated words, phrases and numbers. It was all about controlling me, so I never questioned them or told anyone about who they were and what they were doing.

I lived in constant fear. I couldn't walk down the street without feeling like I was being watched. I couldn't be near cats and kept my fingernails short, which I later attributed as triggers of my first days witnessing the cruelty of the cult and being held captive in the dirt hole.

❧❧❧❧

After graduating from high school, I started Bible college in the fall. I grew up going to church and had accepted Jesus into my heart when I was only 5 years old. Throughout my life, I tried to stay close to Jesus. I tried to trust in him that I could keep my distance from the evil that lurked and the evildoers who wanted me for themselves. I grew up in a loving Christian home, always attending church with my family. My parents loved me and would've been horrified to know the pain I was suffering. I wanted to stay close to God and wanted Bible school to be the first step I took in my adult life.

When I started Bible college, there was a girl named

Laura who lived on the same floor of my dorm who, in retrospect, I suspected was part of the cult network that had abducted me. She watched me a lot. We weren't friends, and yet she was always nearby and consistently paying attention to where I was and what I was doing.

One night, I returned to my dorm room, and there was a bright red spot on my bed. I couldn't tell what it was at first, but as I approached the bed, it became abundantly clear that it was, indeed, blood. It scared me to death. Just then, I heard an odd-sounding scream that seemed to be coming from Laura's room behind her closed door, so my friends and I immediately went to our floor monitor's apartment to tell her about what I'd seen and heard.

"Can you tell me where the sound is coming from?" she asked. "Any of you?" None of us wanted to say that we thought the noise was coming from Laura's room, so we stood silent. "Just be careful, and stay together," she told us.

We had been warned about not going anywhere alone because our Bible college was near the cult headquarters. Every year people would gather during Halloween, and strange and eerie things would happen without explanation. We were warned multiple times to stay in at night and use the buddy system when going anywhere. Still, no one knew of my involvement, and I remained silent about just how real the warnings were.

I never saw Laura again and didn't know where she'd gone. It was a mystery I didn't want to solve.

⇜⇜⇜

I started dating Kurt during my senior year in high school, and we went to Bible college together the fall after I graduated. One weekend Kurt was out of town, and I didn't want to go to church alone, so I decided to ride with a group of people.

When we arrived in front of a big house and not at our church, I felt the uneasiness mounting as my heart began to race from the familiarity of another big house. I tried not to panic because I knew there were people who gathered at houses rather than churches sometimes, so I went inside.

There were about 75 people sitting in chairs that were lined up like a church service, but it didn't feel like a church service. It was a change-of-hands service, which I recognized as various people of the cult organization changing over from one group to another. It was an initiation-type meeting that was very scary to me. It brought back memories of my encounters with the cult over the years, and I wanted to leave. I stayed until it was over because I didn't want to draw attention to myself, and I still feared what might happen to me if I wasn't careful. Fear was my constant companion.

⇜⇜⇜

Kurt and I got married and moved out of the city during our first year of school.

"I can't explain it to you, but I'm just not ready," I told him when it was time to discuss having children.

He knew there were oddities about me, and he often commented on my seeming to think that I had to earn my salvation and do things to make God love me, but I couldn't explain why I was terrified to have children. Later, I understood that the cult had controlled me with fear most of my life and that somehow I must have known that having a child would just magnify that fear. I didn't want to love or risk one more life that I would be responsible for keeping safe.

&smaller;&smaller;&smaller;

As much as my relationship with God was real to me, I still questioned God. Later, I realized that the cult had mixed religious figures, scriptures and deities to destroy my ability to make a healthy connection with God and Jesus. As I recovered my memories of what the cult taught, I realized I'd been convinced by them that Jesus was mad at me and against me. I spent a great deal of time repenting at the altar while I was growing up, asking forgiveness for every little thing I ever did, even if it wasn't something that needed repenting. I felt certain that if I ever made it to heaven, there would surely be a trap door that I would fall in because I fell short of what God wanted from me in my lifetime. I thought it was my fault that the cult had chosen me. I feared the cult, and I feared God.

Kurt and I were married nearly 10 years when we had our first child. When our children were born, I didn't let them leave the room from the time they were born from my body. I didn't trust anyone in the hospital to be who they said they were. I needed to have my babies next to me. Later, I realized I feared the cult would try to come take them from me or send someone to scare me just by being around the hospital or in the parking lot as we left the hospital to go home.

God gave Kurt the strength he needed to endure a life with me. Eventually, I confided in him some of the fears I had about keeping our babies safe in general, but I couldn't tell him why. Again, I couldn't bear the thought of something happening to him. But I rested in his strength and loved him and trusted him beyond measure. He loved our children and loved me and would protect us all, no matter what, even if he was unaware of what he was protecting us from.

Despite Kurt's love and patience, it wasn't always easy for me to receive Kurt's pure love.

"I'm just calling to tell you I love you," Kurt would say to me.

I didn't understand it. I didn't get how he could love me in such a simple way and profess that love without question. There were times when I felt unworthy of the love Kurt showed me. I kept thinking about the horrible things I had witnessed. Logically, I knew I had been brainwashed with fear, but I still blamed myself. I often considered the baby I recalled being told I was responsible for all those years ago who was now grown and still relied on me to stay safe.

After our second child was born, I felt like God started speaking to me, also professing his love for me.

Who knows the heart? I, the Lord, I know your heart, he seemed to say. *I know your motives. I know why you think the way you think.*

You can look into my heart and know my heart? That terrifies me.

I wanted to run. But God steadied me. Little by little.

When I found you in the thicket, you looked at me terrified with your big brown eyes. And you thought when I looked at you, that I would say, "I was looking for somebody, but it wasn't you." And you thought I was just walking away. Isn't that true? I felt God ask me.

If I tell God the truth — the fear that is in my heart — he's God; he's going to kill me. He has that ability. He can wipe my life out. If I lie to him, he already knows my heart. He'll know I'm lying. What do I say?

It can't get any worse than death.

"Yes, it's true," I confessed to God, as tears streamed down my face. Incredibly, I could feel God's full heart of love pour over me. In my mind, God lifted me from the thicket and placed me where I could see the cross over a vast number of people.

If you were there the day I died on the cross, and I looked out into the crowd, you'd think I'd point to people and say, "I died for you and you and you and you." And you'd think, if I pointed to you, I'd say, "I died for him and for her and for him and her," pointing to each person, but you just happened to be at the right place at the right time, so I'll just take you on, I felt God declare. *Isn't that true?*

What I heard God ask was right. I thought I didn't matter.

Suddenly, the scriptures I had read all of my life that I didn't understand were jumping from the page and saying to me, *You didn't choose me, I chose you.*

Oh, sweet Jesus, if I were the only person on earth, you would've died just for me.

❧❧❧

I decided to attend a women's retreat and asked God to help guide me while I was there.

I am needing something from you, God. I need to feel the love of my husband. I need to feel like I am home when I am there, not like I could be thrown in a field down the road and feel just the same there as I do under the roof I share with my family.

There was a wonderful woman at the retreat who was talking about relationships and God's love for us. I cried throughout her whole talk the first night.

"You know what, Becky? I think you have a big heart, and you're someone who really loves people. If someone offends, you forgive him or her right away, but you can't seem to forgive yourself," she said to me when I approached her about being moved by what she'd shared and how I felt unable to receive the love that I was learning I deserved. "My suggestion is that you find a room, and be by yourself, and just talk to yourself. If there is something that you haven't forgiven yourself for, I think you're going to find someone inside yourself who isn't as bad as you think she is and deserves your forgiveness, too."

I did as she suggested and found a room to be alone. As I considered the things I had seen and experienced, I realized I felt enormous guilt. I spent the entire night talking to God and sobbing to him. At one point, I felt like God directed me to look in the mirror to truly see myself. I heard him tell me to list the things that I didn't like about myself, and that's exactly what I did. By morning, after praying and crying throughout the night, a light turned on as I finally understood that I owed myself as much love and forgiveness as I'd given to others. As I said those words and felt their power, I felt new as I looked in the mirror one final time before leaving the room.

You are not the dirty dog I always thought you were. I have met a friend.

When I got home, my husband had gone to his parents' house and left me a card on the table. On the front of the card was a clothesline with clothespins and little birds sitting on the clothespins. The front read, "I love you," and the inside read, "And that's the bottom line."

I grabbed the card and drove straight to his mom and dad's house to greet him. I wrapped my arms around him, still holding the card in my hand, and said, "I accept this. I receive your love."

When I came home, I felt like I had a home. I felt

peace and knew that my relationship with God was not about working for it. A little song played cheerfully in my head, "Jesus loves me, this I know, for the Bible tells me so."

❧❧❧❧

Our home was filled with undeniable love for many years. We started building a house and were managing to build it debt-free. The year after our youngest child was born, Kurt started experiencing unexplained weight loss and, within weeks, was diagnosed with cancer.

"I think we need to sell the house," he told me. "We don't have the money to finish it."

"No, there has to be another way," I insisted.

God must have found a way, because Kurt's boss offered to loan us the money we needed to finish the house. He'd asked Kurt for a dollar amount, so we figured out how much we thought it would cost and that ended up being exactly the amount it cost us to finish — to the penny. Soon after, Kurt had surgery, and we moved into our house. Just five months later, Kurt lost his battle with cancer. He died at home. I can't help but believe that after his death, he went to his eternal home to be with God.

Learning to live without Kurt would've been nearly impossible for me had I not found a church home at New Hope Community Church after he died. Some of my deepest healing from fear and my break from feeling controlled by the cult came after I became involved at New

Hope. My pastor and a professor friend in a nearby town were instrumental in helping me find total freedom from the power and control of the cult. The true healing began when I let Jesus set me free from the cult. And freedom is exactly what I felt.

Through my healing and research as a survivor of satanic ritual abuse, I concluded that my uncle Steve must have used me to replace his own daughter's involvement in the cult of his neighbors. If I was available to them, Abby no longer had to be — I was replacing Abby. Maybe my uncle didn't feel like he had a better option, but understanding that possibility actually reassured me that my selection had nothing to do with me. I was probably doomed from the moment it was decided I would spend a week visiting my uncle and extended family.

Thankfully, my church family at New Hope has been open to my healing process, never making me feel ashamed or unworthy of the forgiveness I now feel in the depths of my soul. I am truly free at last. Kurt had been my protector and the one who loved me unconditionally, but so had God. I had never been alone, and I trust I never will be alone.

After Kurt died, I received just enough life insurance money to repay his boss for the loan he gave us to finish the house. Kurt helped build and died in the house we built together. For years I never felt like I belonged and that nowhere I lived would feel like home. Years later, in the absence of Kurt and in the presence of God, I found my way home — until God takes me to the home I believe he's made for me in heaven. There, I trust we'll all be reunited once again.

I believe it's God's promise to me that there's nothing to fear and that he loves me.

NOWHERE TO GO
THE STORY OF LEIGH
WRITTEN BY ELLEN R. HALE

I locked myself in my bathroom and glanced at the window. My husband, Steve, and his buddy had returned to our apartment after a night of drinking. After Steve passed out, Aaron began pounding on the bathroom door. Knowing full well what he wanted, I stayed inside the bathroom, scared but resolute.

Did he think I didn't remember?

I might never forget the night he'd shown up at our apartment door.

"I thought I'd go with you to pick up Steve from work tonight," he'd suggested.

"All right, that's fine," I replied. I could tell he had already been drinking.

As we drove from Charlotte out into the country, Aaron asked me to pull off the road so that he could go to the bathroom. I waited for him to come back and return to the passenger's seat. Instead, he opened my door, grabbed my arm and yanked me outside. Then he raped me.

Afterward, I sat behind the wheel, trembling and pulling my jacket back on.

"If you say anything about this to Steve, I'll tell him what you allowed me to do," Aaron warned.

What a lie. I'm not that kind of woman. I would never

run around with other men. I'll never tell Steve this happened. And I won't report it to the police — they always believe these situations are the woman's fault.

So I kept quiet.

Day after day, Aaron walked up and down our street, staring at our apartment. He knocked on our door, but I never dared open it. When my drunken husband brought him home with him, I fled to the bathroom.

If Aaron managed to break down the door, I planned to holler out the window. Maybe, just maybe, our landlord who lived below us or someone else would hear my cries for help.

Terrified, I hoped the lock would keep me safe.

I had nowhere else to go.

❧❧❧

My six siblings and I huddled in a barn and watched through a small hole as military policemen put handcuffs on our father and drove away with him. A relative had turned him in for going AWOL.

His arrest left my mother to care for seven children in a tiny house with only three rooms. All of us shared one bedroom and slept in cribs, cold and hungry. My father had been an alcoholic, and I dreaded hearing him yell at my mother in his booming voice.

A teenager was babysitting us when a man arrived at our house and ordered me into his car. I was 3 years old. After driving for what seemed liked miles and miles, we pulled up to a farm — a foster home. As we approached the back porch, I saw dead chickens being dipped in boiling water to remove their feathers. I remember feeling afraid and confused.

Where am I? Where are my parents and siblings? Who are these strangers?

At night, I lay alone in a bedroom, unable to sleep. The foster parents' daughter — a blond girl who was older than me — enjoyed picking on me by pulling my tangled hair, which was black like my mother's.

Just after I turned 4, the authorities came and placed me in a different foster home.

"Daddy!" I cried when I saw the tall, thin man who looked like my father. But again, I felt confused because the woman clearly was not my mother — she didn't have my mother's black hair.

On their farm, my new parents quickly put me to work. They owned chickens, cattle, horses and other animals. That harvest season, I rode on a tractor in the fields with my foster father. His brother and his brother's teenage son often came to our farm to assist with the work. Dad sent me to the barn to stomp inside the grain bin and level off the grain. Dust from the operation filled the barn, making it difficult to see or breathe. My cousin followed me inside the barn and grabbed me. Then he did other things that scared me and that I didn't begin to understand — I thought he was trying to choke me or kill me.

The way he'd touched me made me feel constantly sick

to my stomach. Almost every night, I vomited in my bed. My foster parents moved me to a rollaway bed in their room so that they could help me when I felt the urge to vomit. They took me to a doctor who prescribed a medication for my stomach problems.

My loneliness decreased slightly when my foster parents decided to take in one of my brothers and adopt both of us. Michael and I started school, but he suffered from a speech impediment, and I dealt with a learning disability. I muddled through reading, spelling and math.

In addition, my classmates teased me for being overweight. When Michael and I weren't in school, our parents had a never-ending list of chores for us to do. We awoke early to feed animals before the school bus arrived, and we returned to our tasks when the bus dropped us off after school. Some days, Dad kept us home from school to bale hay. Once I was old enough, my mother asked me to do indoor chores, like cooking and washing dishes, too. It didn't seem fair — we never had time for any fun like other kids did.

By the time I was 12, I enjoyed dancing at school with my friends in the gym after lunch. The elementary and high school students all attended the same school, and a boy who was older than me noticed me dancing.

One day, he followed me off the school bus, and his friend pulled up in his car at my house. I tried to run upstairs to the bathroom, but that boy pushed on the door and raped me. No one had taught me about sex, so I still didn't understand what had happened. The assaults left me scarred, physically and emotionally, and thinking I would die.

My adoptive family attended church regularly, and that became my only escape from school and chores. I wished that Sunday school or Vacation Bible School took place every day.

"This little light of mine, I'm gonna let it shine," we sang in Sunday school. "Let it shine, let it shine, let it shine." The teachers told us the story of a young boy in another country who didn't have a family. They collected money to send him, and I eagerly gave my pennies to the cause. I loved hearing our teachers read letters from the boy. I grew to view him as a friend who understood a bit of the hurt and fear I felt after being taken from my biological family.

During a service at a church one of my friends attended, I embraced Jesus as my friend and believed that he would listen to the troubles I didn't dare share with anyone else. "Lord," I'd pray, "please help me understand what is going on. Where is the rest of my family? Where is my mother?"

෨෨෨

Our neighbors were watching my brother and me at their home one summer day when a man knocked on their door. We had seen him driving a station wagon with wood paneling up and down the dirt road past our house, and we thought he was a stalker. But he grasped a photograph of Michael, who had dropped out of school, and wanted to know where he was. My brother met him outside.

"I'm your dad," the man said. They looked exactly alike, but Michael responded with anger.

"No!" he yelled as he tackled the man. "My dad's dead. You're not my father!" Someone managed to pull the two apart.

The man grew increasingly insistent in his efforts to reach us. And increasingly violent. Our phone rang in the middle of the night. He held Eaton County deputies at gunpoint, demanding to speak to me. I shuffled out of bed and tried to calm down the drunken man.

"They had no right to take you," he insisted. "You're my child, and I was in prison." I began to wonder if we *had* been taken illegally.

One day, he arrived at the farm and pointed his shotgun at us, ordering Michael and me into the station wagon. Michael told me to return to the house.

"If you're going to shoot someone, shoot me," he challenged. "But you're not going to shoot my sister."

Finally, we attended a court hearing.

"Yes, this is your father," the judge explained. "You were taken away from him, and his home is not a place you want to go back to." I was about 14 years old.

"Leave me alone," I pleaded with my father. "When I'm 18, I will come and see you someday. But I can't do that now. I need to stay where I am."

❧❧❧

I started driving at 14 and had a 10 p.m. curfew. I loved cruising in Lansing, Eaton Rapids or Grand Ledge. I exchanged phone numbers with a boy named Steve who was two years older than me. We began dating, and he proposed during my junior year. My senior year, I would walk to his job in Charlotte after school each day.

"I think I'll go home on the bus," I told Steve over lunch one April day. "I'm not feeling that well."

At home, I saw a car pull up, and a funeral home director approached the door.

"Are your parents home?" he asked.

Before I could answer him, the phone rang. My parents were calling. I turned the phone over to the funeral home director who informed my parents they needed to come home right away. My brother, who worked in Lansing, had been killed in an accident with a tractor-trailer.

Grief overwhelmed me. Michael was the only blood relative who had been with me through my life. We shared the same experiences, making us extremely close. And just like that, he was gone.

I battled to finish school and graduate in June. Then in September, my birth father died from complications of his alcoholism. I didn't keep my promise to visit him and get to know him once I turned 18. Even after he died, I walked right past the funeral home and didn't stop to pay my respects.

Meanwhile, I planned a December wedding to Steve at a Methodist church. After joining the National Guard,

Steve began drinking at bars and on the job. Similar to my birth father, my drunken husband yelled loudly and sometimes pushed or shoved me. He regularly lost jobs because of his drinking.

I decided to meet my birth mother, whose presence I greatly missed. I couldn't believe my eyes. She sat on a man's lap, and younger sisters I had never met looked like prostitutes. Older men filled the house.

"People don't live like this," I told my mother. I cried the entire drive back to my apartment, feeling guilty about their living conditions compared to mine.

It's terrible the way these kids are living. I feel so bad for them, but I don't know what to do. I've had a hard time as an adopted child, but I've actually had a better life than my siblings who stayed with my mom.

When one of my sisters ended up pregnant at 14, I let her live with Steve and me in our apartment. I'd work during the day and help her with the new baby at night.

The night Aaron raped me occurred after she and the baby moved out — only a year after my wedding. Later, my adoptive parents moved from their farm to Lansing, so Steve and I moved from our apartment back to the farm where I grew up. I kept busy taking care of others. Since Steve and I didn't have children, I obtained certification as a foster mother myself and fostered several children during the next two years.

I believed that having a child of our own would save my marriage to Steve. We had been married 10 years without a pregnancy.

I consulted my doctor, who discovered that both of my fallopian tubes were blocked, causing infertility. After he fixed the blockage on one side and prescribed medication for me, I became pregnant in three months. But Steve's alcoholism continued after the birth of our daughter and later our sons. I contemplated divorce, but I stayed with him because of our children. I dreamed he would change someday.

My adoptive mother developed Alzheimer's disease, and my adoptive father suffered with the effects of a stroke. At one time, I changed diapers not only on my children but also on both my parents.

By the time my children were all in school, the exhaustion from taking care of everyone else left me no longer wanting to live. I eyed a bottle of prescription medication and decided to kill myself by overdosing while my kids were at school.

My daughter caused me to change my plans.

"Mommy, I'm not going to school today. I feel sick."

Then my phone rang. It was my neighbor, who could hear the desperation in my voice. Minutes later, she came over and listened to my struggles. I believe God used her to prevent me from committing suicide. After that, a friend invited me to attend a Presbyterian church. I brought my children and my parents to the services. I recalled how I had turned to Jesus for help as a child. Once again, church became my only time of respite from the hard work of caring for my kids and parents.

Several years later, I suffered a slight heart attack.

"You are not going home unless you find someone to help you with your parents and give you a break from your kids," the doctor ordered. I decided to meet with a counselor for the first time. We talked about how my marriage wasn't working.

My adoptive mother died during the summer, and my adoptive father died the following January. I discussed my next steps with my therapist. She tried to counsel Steve during several sessions, but he didn't change.

"You know in your heart what you need to do," she advised me.

I also spoke with the pastor at the Presbyterian church. "I married Steve for better or worse, but his alcoholism prevents him from loving or supporting me in any way." The pastor prayed with me.

"This is not the kind of life the Lord wants you to have," he told me. "Steve is not doing what the Bible says he should do for you and your children."

I met with a divorce attorney. He advised me to finalize the divorce first and then settle my parents' estate to protect me from Steve's financial demands. He wanted the entire estate. In 24 years of marriage, he had worked 32 different jobs. He loved alcohol more than anyone or anything.

After my divorce, I learned that my birth mother had been diagnosed with chronic obstructive pulmonary disease, even though she didn't smoke.

I made an effort to get to know her better. I realized that the constant abuse she endured from my father and other men deeply affected her ability to improve her circumstances. I understood her perspective — that she couldn't stop getting pregnant, and she couldn't fight to keep her children and care for them appropriately. My father had once told a judge, "You took our seven children — we will have seven more!" Before my mother died, I managed to forgive her, even if I couldn't forget what it felt like to go through my childhood without her.

ॐ ॐ ॐ

"I'm seeing somebody else." I couldn't believe my ears. Joe and I had been together for 20 years — when he wasn't in jail for drunken driving. When he'd get out, he always promised to stop drinking but never sought treatment.

Although we weren't living together, he frequently spent the night at my place. That stopped, however, when I had surgery to repair a hernia. The doctors planned it as an outpatient procedure, but I stopped breathing, and they needed to resuscitate me. I stayed in the hospital for two days while the doctors worked to increase my oxygen level. Joe didn't visit me in the hospital or after my release, and I decided to find out why. His admission stunned me. How could Joe reject me after I'd stood by him for two decades?

I sat at home, alone and tired. My children were adults with their own children. I saw no escape from my lifetime of trials. My relationships with men always ended in failure. Thoughts of suicide again filled my mind.

Then my grandchildren invited me to a special event at New Hope Community Church. They had heard Christian bodybuilders speak at their school and asked me to come listen when the bodybuilders gave another presentation at New Hope. While at the church, I spotted information on the bulletin board about a chapter of the Red Hat Society, a social organization for women. It interested me. I decided to attend a service.

I sat by myself. When the time came for the sermon, they projected Bible verses on a large screen while Pastor Randy spoke. In addition, I easily followed along using a guide printed in the bulletin. *What a surprise. My learning disability always made it difficult for me to understand the teaching at the churches I attended before because I spent all my time searching my Bible for various verses. New Hope is making it easy for me to learn more about Jesus.*

My childlike belief in Jesus grew as I worshipped at New Hope each week. I found the music uplifting and the people welcoming. I formed friendships with some of the ladies at New Hope. *Could this church be the loving home I've longed for my entire life?*

I attended churches in the past but never became a member. I believed in Jesus, but that never affected how I lived. I chose to take New Hope's membership class, and I learned about the church's beliefs and my role in the church.

For about two years, I met with a counselor I met through someone at church. I finally opened up to my counselor about how men mistreated me my entire life and how I mourned growing up apart from my birth family, particularly my mother. I faced feelings I held inside for so long, such as the agony I felt when Aaron raped me. I came to realize how much being born into an alcoholic family affected me, my siblings and my children. Facing this with God's help healed my deep hurts, and I experienced a feeling of freedom.

Looking back on my life, I realized that God never left me. I did pray to Jesus as a little girl, but I finally came to have a personal relationship with him. That has made a huge difference. I read my Bible at home and pray to the Lord — not only for others but also for the strength I need to live each day.

I started spending as much time as possible at New Hope and base my schedule around the services and other activities. Sometimes I feel lonesome, but Jesus keeps me company day in and day out. I want to serve him in any way I can and assist those in need. I'm not afraid to encourage others by telling them that God loves them. I never know when someone I meet is like I had been my whole life — hiding significant pain behind a smile and needing to hear words of hope.

☙☙☙

One of Joe's sons developed cancer and received a bone marrow transplant from a sibling.

"I'm praying for you," I told Scott as he fought through his chemotherapy treatments.

He put up his hand to stop me. He didn't believe in

Jesus and didn't want to hear any more from me. The doctors eventually declared him free of cancer.

Scott later complained of back problems. The doctors discovered a tumor and performed surgery to remove it, and fortunately the growth wasn't cancerous. Several months passed, and his back trouble returned. A biopsy revealed cancer from the top of his neck to the bottom of his spine. The doctors reported that no treatment existed and estimated that Scott would not live more than two weeks. The only prescription was hospice care.

I asked Pastor Randy to visit him, thinking maybe Scott would listen to someone who had experience talking to people who were facing death. But before Pastor Randy came, I wanted to tell Scott to expect his visit.

The simple words I sang in Sunday school as a confused little girl returned to my mind: "This little light of mine, I'm gonna let it shine. Let it shine, let it shine, let it shine."

I walked into Scott's room, sat down and placed my hand on his. He could barely speak.

"You might be upset with me, but I've asked my minister to come visit you tomorrow. Please be nice to him. Scott, I know I'm going to heaven, and I want you to be there, too. For 25 years, you've called to wish me a happy Mother's Day. I'm going to miss that. You're getting to the end of your time. What are you going to say when my pastor asks if you want Jesus to forgive you for your mistakes and be your Savior? Are you going to do that?"

"Yes." Scott nodded, and his face immediately brightened. "I hear music," he whispered. "I'm dancing."

He closed his eyes, and I left him to sleep. In the morning, I found out that Scott never woke up again. He died a few hours after I departed.

"Pastor Randy didn't get a chance to visit him," I told my counselor, concern in my voice.

"He didn't have to. You told Scott what he needed to do to go to heaven. He answered you."

And so, I believe that Scott is in heaven with Jesus. I believe God used me to reach Scott just before he died. I consider that a miracle — one that wouldn't have been possible before I found somewhere to go, a home I can never lose and a family that will never fail me.

WAITING
THE STORY OF MICHELE ROYSTON
WRITTEN BY MELISSA HARDING

"What would you like us to do, Michele?"

The doctor's words confused me, my brain scrambling to understand their meaning. The room swayed like a ship at sea. *What happened? Where am I?* Thoughts flashed across the landscape of my mind as pain seared through my abdomen. *Ah, yes ... the hospital ... contractions ... doctors' faces ... blood ... so much blood.* My hands went to my belly, but the seven-month bulge I expected to find protruding from my body wasn't there. No longer swollen with life, my stomach lay deflated and empty. And then I panicked. *My baby!*

"Where is my baby? I want to see my baby!" I gasped. I recalled someone carrying my son's tiny body away, and my heart sank with grief. He wasn't ready to face the world. He was too little, too weak. He needed more time to develop. I remembered seeing his little feet and hearing the doctors trying to get him to breathe.

Oh, my baby. My sweet little baby. Sorrow swallowed me as my uterus contracted. I yearned to hold my baby in my arms and ached with emptiness.

"Michele, we don't think that's a good idea. We need to know what you want us to do." The doctor's voice reached through my panic, pulling me out of my thoughts and back to reality. "He's alive, but he's struggling to breathe. We can put him on oxygen, but we need to act fast. What do you want?"

Oh, God! I don't know what to do. I'm 19. How could I possibly know what to do?

"I want to see my baby," I cried, my body trembling with determination. "Please let me see my baby."

෨෨෨

I grew up in the '60s, the oldest in a large family. We lived in tight quarters. My four sisters and I shared a bathroom, and as I grew, a fierce desire to protect them rose within me. Because my dad was a pastor, I went to church from the time I was a little girl. I loved learning about God and the Bible. I loved being inside the safe walls of the church. One Sunday night, after the service, I felt something strange inside me. I came home crying, unable to pinpoint what was wrong.

"What's the matter, Michele?" Mom asked when she saw me.

"I don't know. I just feel something in my heart that says I want something more than just going to church."

"Well, have you ever asked Jesus to come and live inside your heart?"

"No. What does that mean?"

"It means that you believe that Jesus died to save you from the wrong things you've done. You ask him to forgive you, and then he comes and lives inside of you always."

"Yes, that's what I want to do!" Excitement welled up within me. I knew from that moment on that I would never be the same.

≈≈≈

Although our home was full and nearly bursting with people, and I rarely had time to myself, I often felt lonely. Sometimes, the loneliness overwhelmed me, and I felt that no one in the world could see me. One day, I ran to the woods, clutching my Bible, the tears streaming down my face.

"Why doesn't anybody love me?" I cried out. "Why doesn't anybody want to be with me?"

I sat under my favorite pine tree, breathing in the silence and beauty surrounding me. Loneliness threatened to break my heart, so I opened my Bible and read, desperate to know that someone cared.

"Will you love me, God?" I whispered, clinging to the promises I read in the Bible.

Yes, my child. I will never leave you or forsake you. The answer I heard in my heart poured over me like balm over a wound. My mind jumbled with confusion. What was real, and what was fake? I went to church, but it didn't always seem like people's lives reflected the things we talked about on Sundays. I figured the best place to find the truth was from God himself. So I read the Bible, and I talked to him like I would talk to a best friend. I believed he talked to me, too, and my love for him grew stronger every day.

❧ ❧ ❧

"Hey, guys! Look out, here comes the nun!" Snickering followed as I walked past a group of kids at my high school. I carried my Bible everywhere, and I didn't care what anyone thought or said about it.

I went to high school in the '70s, when the prevailing free-love mentality of the hippie movement embraced by many of my classmates made both my moral decisions and myself unpopular.

"You can laugh all you want, but someday you're going to see that God is real. You all think that love is free, but love isn't free. It came at a great cost. God loves you, and he sent his son, Jesus, to die for you."

"Yeah, okay, Mother Mary, thank you for the sermon!" More laughter erupted, but it didn't faze my resolve. Convinced that God had his hand on me, I wouldn't waver from the path I believed he laid out before me. I was going to serve him with all my heart, no matter the cost.

Our school consisted of many diverse groups of people. I sat next to a self-professed witch in one of my classes. Knowing my faith in God, she threatened to cast a curse on me.

"I have more powers than you can even believe," she whispered one day, hoping to shake my confidence. "I can cast a curse on you, and then you will know what real power is."

"I wouldn't do that if I were you," I said, looking into her eyes. "I have the power of the living God inside me.

Your curse won't work. Anything you cast on me will end up on you."

While she may have known a supernatural power, she didn't dare trifle with the power I proclaimed.

绐绐绐

I met Randy in seventh grade. We didn't run in the same circles, but we knew each other and became friends over the years. As my love for God grew, I felt him speak to my heart more and more. One night I prayed for direction for my life. I was committed to following God anywhere he wanted me to go, but I wanted to know for sure.

"What do you want me to do with my life, Lord? Just say it, and I'll do it. I want to be the person you made me to be, no matter what."

Michele. An audible voice seemed to echo through the room, resonating in every cell of my body. I looked around, trying to find the source of the voice. I prayed again.

"God, please answer me. I want to serve you. Tell me what you want me to do with my life."

Michele. I heard the voice again. It covered me with a peace and joy I'd never known before. I knew then who must be speaking, and my whole body trembled with excitement.

"Yes, Lord. I'm listening."

You're going to marry Randy. You will go to Bible

school in Minneapolis. It's going to be very hard. He's as stubborn as you are. That's why he needs you. If you will do what I ask, I will make Randy into an incredible pastor, and many lives will be impacted because of him.

Tears poured down my cheeks, and I breathed out, letting go of my fear and doubt.

"Okay," I whispered, strength and joy filling me to the brim.

Michele. The voice spoke to my heart again. *I will never leave you.*

҂҂҂

"Hey, Michele." I felt a light touch on my shoulder. I turned around and looked into Randy's mischievous eyes. He didn't know about my secret with God. But I knew, and I was certain that everything would happen when the timing was right. We took many of the same classes, but nothing more than friendship developed. Other guys began to notice me, though, and I could tell it was making Randy a little jealous.

"Yeah?" I said sweetly.

"Can I see your class ring?" he asked, pointing down at my hand.

"Sure," I said, pulling the ring off my finger and placing it in his hands.

Before I could react, Randy took off running with the ring. I ran after him, and once I finally caught up, he said, "Wanna go out sometime with me?"

I smiled to myself, thinking about God's sense of humor. "Yeah, I'd like that."

"How about Sunday night?"

"Oh, I can't go on Sunday. I have church that night."

"Well, what about Wednesday?"

"No, I have youth group then."

"Wow, seriously? Can't you miss it just once? All the Christians I know are just a bunch of hypocrites. I don't want anything to do with it."

"Well, it means a lot to me. If you want to go out with me, you'll have to understand that."

We settled on another day and slowly began to see each other more and more. Randy liked to drink with his football buddies. I wouldn't let him anywhere near me if he had alcohol on his breath. At first it shocked him that I was so firm in my convictions, but after a while, he began to ask more questions.

"You're really serious about this church stuff, aren't you?" he asked one night on the phone.

"Have you ever wondered why?" I replied, my heart quickening at the possibility of Randy finally understanding who God was and how much God wanted a relationship with him.

"Yeah, but I don't understand. All the Christians I know are worse than me. They party and swear. I just don't see the point."

"It's not about being good, Randy," I said. "My relationship with God is everything to me. You're right, there are a bunch of hypocrites who claim to be

Christians. But what are you going to do about Jesus? Regardless of what other people say and do, someday you will come face-to-face with this question: Who is he, and what does that mean to you?"

"I don't know," he said, sighing. "I know I need something, though. There's a hole inside of me."

"Uh-huh!" I exclaimed. He was finally getting it. "God put that hole there. Only Jesus can fill it."

Silence echoed across the phone line, and then finally Randy said, "Okay, what do I do?"

"Tell God you want to know him. You can't do this alone. You need Jesus. Ask him to forgive you for all the wrong things you've done that separate you from God. Ask Jesus to come and live inside you."

Randy prayed and received Jesus into his life right then. I encouraged him to tell our youth group, and not long after, he was baptized — immersed in water and raised up again — a physical symbol of what God did in his heart.

At 18 years old, I walked down the aisle and pledged my life to Randy. For better or worse, in sickness and in health. Little did we know we would face the worst first.

∝∝∝

I gripped the porcelain bowl and heaved again as my insides retched.

"Why, God?" I asked. I was 19. I didn't want a baby yet. I was so sick, and even after I passed my first trimester, the sickness didn't subside. Every flush was another reminder of my dreams going down the drain. I wanted to wait to have children. Randy and I were newly married, and our whole lives lay before us. This wasn't part of our plan, and I was angry. So was Randy. He wanted to have fun and do things other young people did.

"Come on, Michele. Let's go. I don't want to stay home. Let's go have some fun," Randy cajoled. But I was too sick to do anything. Many nights I spent alone while he partied late into the night with our friends.

"I can't. I feel so awful. Can't we just stay here together?"

"No! I'm sick of sitting around doing nothing! We should be out there living life!"

Randy was the man of our house, and although I knew he loved me, after we got married, the fire of love that once blazed between us began to fizzle. As the baby grew within me, Randy and I grew further and further apart. The emotional distance devastated me, and my heart ached as my belly stretched. I didn't even recognize that wide-eyed girl who'd walked down the aisle to join hands with the man of her dreams just a short time before.

Oh, God. What do I do? Why do I have to do this?

Michele, this child is a gift. The sweet whisper spoke to my aching heart, wrapping around me like a gentle embrace. I looked down at my stomach and trailed my fingers across the tender skin. I felt the baby move, like ripples across the water, and stared in amazement at the tiny miracle forming within me. I imagined who this child would be and the lifetime of moments he would know.

A gift? I knew right then and there that this baby would forever change my life.

తతతత

Pain shot through my stomach and jolted me awake. I looked at the clock and groaned — 1 a.m. I lay back down and tried to relax, but a few minutes later, another pain seared through my side. Something was wrong. I was only seven months along. The baby wasn't ready. It wasn't time. My stomach felt like a tight fist, releasing for a few minutes, then tightening again.

"Randy," I heaved. "Something's wrong. I need to go see my mom."

We drove to my parents' house, and the second my mom saw me, she said, "You're in labor. We've gotta get you to the hospital."

My dad drove, while my mom timed my contractions. "Hurry, they're three minutes apart," she cried. "We don't have much time."

God, I meant what I said. I squeezed my eyes shut as my abdomen tightened again. *Help me!*

When we arrived at the hospital, I got out of the car and heard a splash. I looked down, and the ground at my feet was covered in blood. The nurse at registration leaped over the desk and called for a gurney. Everything grew fuzzy and began to spin. I didn't know what was happening. When I opened my eyes, I saw doctors and nurses putting in IVs, talking in low voices. And I saw so much blood.

Randy stayed beside me, his eyes wide with fear and uncertainty. I looked at his worried face. He was so young. Neither of us had a clue what was going on or what to do. The doctor's voice was gentle but strained.

"Well, Mr. and Mrs. Royston, you are in labor. I have some bad news, though. Michele, you are dying. You've lost too much blood. Both you and the baby won't survive. I'm so sorry to tell you this, but it's one of you or the other."

I heard my mom scream through the window glass, "Save my daughter!"

My motherly instincts pushed past my fear, and I shouted, "Save my baby!"

Suddenly, the room began to spin, and my mind drifted out of consciousness. As if I were taking off my clothes, I had the sensation of moving outside of my body and stepping into the hallway.

Is this a dream?

I recall standing in a narrow corridor, lined with doors. A light flashed at the end of the hallway, and I began moving toward it. Voices beckoned me from behind the doors, but I couldn't take my eyes off the light.

I somehow knew the light was Jesus. As I recall it, he stretched out his arms to me and said, "Michele, the baby isn't going to make it. I'm taking him home."

"Can't we both come?" I asked.

"No, Michele. You still have a job to do here. You have to stay."

The vision morphed, sending me back into an urgent

reality, and I screamed with the intensity of my contractions. While I'd been unconscious, the doctors' hope grew that both the baby and I might survive. They pushed me into a delivery room, and my body prepared to bring a tiny life into this world.

"You've got this, Michele. You're doing great." Randy pushed my hair back and trailed his fingers across my tired face. "I'll get the baby's bed ready."

I took his hand and gripped it with all the strength I had left. "No, honey. He's not coming home," I said through my tears.

The next several minutes passed like a whirlwind, my mind fading in and out of consciousness. The baby came, but no sound of crying followed. The slap of hands against a tiny body resounded in my ears like a clock ticking down the seconds. *Breathe!* I screamed silently.

"Please let me see him," I begged a nurse.

No one heard my plea as the doctor rushed past me with my baby in his arms. *No!* my heart cried. I fought against the oxygen mask over my face, but I couldn't hold on any longer. Letting go, I succumbed once again to unconsciousness.

পপপপ

Squinting, I looked around at the room, the lights beckoning me back to reality. *Where was I? What happened?*

"What would you like us to do, Michele?" The doctor's

words broke through my haze, and a deep ache formed in my chest. My hands felt my belly, once swollen with life. Like a deflated balloon, the hollow shell twinged with longing.

"Your baby is alive, Michele, but he's barely hanging on. He's struggling to breathe. He's fighting for each breath right now. We need to know what you want us to do. Do you want us to put him on oxygen or let him go?"

What do I do? I panicked. I didn't know how to make decisions like this. Suddenly, the desire to see my baby welled within me. All I wanted was to see him. To hold him.

"Can I see him?"

"We don't think that's a good idea. It's going to be very difficult."

"I don't care. I want to see him. You have to let me see my baby. That's what I want," I demanded.

They brought the tiny bundle to me, and my arms enveloped him like a cocoon. One look at his beautiful face and my heart melted. I held him close and ran my fingers across his silky skin. He was perfect. His breathing steadied, and for a moment I imagined him growing up like other little boys — climbing trees, getting into mischief, trying my patience and stealing my heart.

Jason. My sweet little boy. I kissed his forehead, drinking in his baby smell.

Oh, God! What do you want me to do? I wanted to hold this treasure in my arms forever. I wanted to watch him grow up. I wanted to never let go.

As I prayed, asking God to show me his will, I began to dream again. I saw the walls of the hospital room open like a scroll. In my vision, a little boy stood at the bottom of a grassy hill. He was blind, and he was wearing an oxygen mask. His little body trembled as tears poured down his face. Realizing it was Jason, I gripped his hand tightly, not wanting to let go. I looked up at the top of the hill and saw Jesus smiling at Jason and waving for him to come up. Kids rolled in the grass, their laughter floating across the wind.

"Mommy, can I go and play?" Jason looked up at me, but I couldn't let go. *How could I let my baby go?*

A voice surrounded me like a warm blanket, and a calm assurance settled over me. *Michele,* the voice called. *Let go of his hand, and let him come home.*

I looked down again at my sweet little boy as he struggled to breathe and looked up at the children playing on the hill. Then I knew what I needed to do.

"Okay, sweetie. You can go." I let go of Jason's hand and watched as he raced into the arms of Jesus.

"What do you want us to do?" The grassy hill faded, and I found myself once again looking at the hospital room. The doctor's words jolted me to the present, and I knew what I needed to do.

"He wants to go home," I said, my heart breaking.

"Okay, let's put him on oxygen, then." The doctor leaned down to take the baby.

"No, he's going home to heaven," I said through my tears.

WAITING

৵৵৵

As I climbed into the car, both my belly and arms empty, grief crashed into me like a tidal wave. The doctors didn't think it was best for me to attend the funeral, so Randy went alone. He came back once it was over, and the doctors discharged me from the hospital. A body that gives birth doesn't know if the baby comes home or not. My chest ached, and my heart throbbed. Nobody knew how to deal with the grief we all felt, so nobody said anything. I felt like I wasn't allowed to talk about Jason. It seemed like to everyone else he never existed. But my aching body and heart couldn't forget. Randy didn't know how to handle a wife who cried all the time, so he withdrew further and further away. As we drifted apart, he came home less. He worked in a factory during the day, but he often found reasons to stay away and didn't return home until late into the night.

"Can you please just stay home?" I cried in desperation one night. "Can we please talk?"

"No," he answered and walked out the door.

Loneliness became my closest companion. Like quicksand, it pulled me in deeper and deeper, until I became unable to find my way out. Depression followed me like a storm cloud. Family members encouraged us to have another baby. To me, their words sounded like taunts, like a pounding gong in my mind: *You're not really a family until you have children. He's going to leave you for someone who can give him children if you don't hurry up and do something.* I couldn't escape what felt like incessant reminders of my failures and disappointments. Even after time passed, easing the intensity of my agony and grief, even once I could consider the possibility of more children — even then, I couldn't get pregnant. The months passed, but my womb remained a barren wilderness, void of life. I looked at my life and felt hopelessness threaten to consume me. An empty womb, a marriage dangling by a thread and nowhere to find support. *What did I have left?*

The only place I knew to turn was to God. That day in high school, I heard him promise he would never leave me. I gripped that promise like a lifesaver and let God pull me out of my sea of despair. Maybe I couldn't talk about Jason to the people in my life, but I could talk to God about him for hours. As I poured out my sorrow to my heavenly father, I found strength in feeling his strong embrace. I found hope in trusting his never-failing love. And I found enough light in sensing his presence to guide my every step. I still believed that God meant for Randy to become a pastor and that someday it would come true. *But how?* Randy had no desire to become a pastor. I trusted, though, that it would happen in God's timing, not mine.

In those months of heartbreak, I clung to God's promises in the Bible. He spoke to me through the Bible and reminded me of his love for me. If I would only wait on him, he would indeed give me the strength to make it through each day. I have learned that as we grow in Christ, he teaches us to grow in his word, the word he left us in the Bible. I drank his words in as if my life depended on them. Like honey on my tongue, they were sweet and satisfying. They filled my hungry soul with nourishment and hope.

"God, show him!" I prayed. "Show Randy your plans for him. Make yourself real, and draw him to yourself. I will wait on you. I believe that you have good things in store for me and my marriage."

Once again, peace flooded my heart. I didn't need to know precisely what would happen in the future.

I believe God gave me just enough light to see where I was standing, and that was enough. I could trust him with every piece of my life. Joy welled up within me, and I knew I could face whatever lay ahead with God there to strengthen me.

ᏯᏭᏯ

I sat in the back of the church, the dim lights of the sanctuary dancing across the faces of people young and old. Randy sat in front, and as the music began, I felt a stirring within me. God was up to something, I realized, and my skin tingled with excitement. I strained my neck to look at Randy, and I could tell something was different.

"Speak to him, Lord," I whispered.

Tonight is the night, he seemed to whisper back.

The pastor stood before the church, inviting people to come down and receive prayer. Randy moved forward and prayed by himself, while the pastor prayed with a group to the side. Suddenly, the pastor stopped and looked over at Randy. He walked over to him, placed his hand on his right shoulder and began praying. I could see Randy's shoulders shaking, and I knew the time had finally come.

I leaned over to my mom sitting beside me and said, "Mom, we're going into the ministry." Her eyes grew wide, and she smiled as understanding dawned.

Later that night, Randy took me aside, trembling with excitement. "Michele, I need to talk with you about what happened tonight."

I smiled and waited for him to tell me what I already knew.

"As I knelt praying, I felt God say to me, *Randy, you're going to be a pastor.* I couldn't believe my ears. Me? A pastor? I'm so shy, and the thought of standing up in front of people and speaking turns my legs into Jell-O! I'm tired of running, though. I want to follow God's plan for my life from now on and not my own. I wanted to make sure I heard him right, so I said I needed some confirmation. I said, 'If that's really you, God, then prompt the pastor to come over here and place his hand on my right shoulder.' That's exactly what he did!" He took my hands and brought them to his chest. "I'm going to be a pastor, Michele! Are you ready to go on a wild adventure with me?"

A new light shone in Randy's eyes. We moved Minneapolis to attend Bible school, and God began to mend the tattered shreds of our hearts back together. We were becoming one in body, mind and spirit.

WAITING

꙳꙳꙳

Randy finished his last year of Bible school, and we moved to South Dakota where Randy began his ministry as a pastor.

I smiled to myself, thinking back on God's promise to me so many years before. If I'd controlled the timing, it would have happened long before. But seeing Randy follow God himself made it all worthwhile. Had I jumped in and tried to out-run God, I wouldn't have had the privilege of watching God transform Randy into the passionate man he has become. One thing clouded our joy, though. After years of trying, there still was no baby. We started fertility treatments, but no baby filled my womb. In moments of frustration, I cried out to God for answers.

"Why, God? Why can't I get pregnant? Please give us a baby," I begged.

We decided to visit another fertility specialist. She suggested that we pursue a sperm donor if we really wanted to get pregnant. My heart plummeted. A donor? Was that what God wanted for us? It just didn't feel right.

Confident that God still had something up his sleeve for us, I turned to her and said, "No, I'll get pregnant when God wants me to, and it will be with my husband."

We began the adoption process, and the wait began. The days turned into weeks, and we waited for the phone call that would fill our empty arms with a baby. The day finally arrived, and our agency called to tell us they had a baby waiting for us to take home. There were some things they needed to check out first, though, so the waiting game continued.

In the meantime, Randy felt God calling us to Michigan. I hadn't felt well in weeks, unable to shake a bout of flu, but we packed up our home and prepared for our move to Michigan. The flu continued to rack my body, and I continually threw up most of my meals. I grew concerned and finally went to see the doctor.

"Well, Mrs. Royston, it looks like you don't have the flu. Your pregnancy test is positive."

"I am not pregnant," I said, unprepared for his words.

"Okay, well, can I check you, anyway?" he asked, a slight grin pulling at his lips.

"Sure, but I know I'm not pregnant," I replied.

"For not being pregnant, I'd guess you're nine weeks along."

"No, I'm not." It didn't matter what the test said. It didn't matter what my uterus looked like. I couldn't believe that I was pregnant.

We moved to Michigan, but my body continued to fight what I still believed was a flu waging war in my stomach. Randy finally said, "This can't be the flu. We're taking you to the doctor."

After looking at my blood tests, the doctor looked up with a smile and said, "You are most definitely pregnant, Mrs. Royston."

Randy jumped out of his chair, fury on his face. "Don't tell her that. She's been hurt enough."

WAITING

I was pregnant. I finally accepted it was true. I was three and a half months pregnant.

That same day, someone from the adoption agency called. They'd finally settled our case. In three days, we would pick up our long-awaited son.

All I could think was, *God certainly has a sense of humor.*

෨෨෨

I looked down into Nathan's brown eyes and melted. My doctor advised me not to lift more than 20 pounds, so I sat in the hotel chair to hold my son for the first time. When someone placed him in my arms, I knew in that moment that the long wait was over. He was mine, and he was everything I had dreamed of and more.

"Hi, honey," I whispered, breathing in his sweet scent.

He looked up into my eyes, smiled and carried my heart away.

The social worker observed us and exclaimed, "Looks like you've been ready for this for a long time."

I sighed and replied, "Oh, you have no idea."

Eric was born a few months later, and the two boys filled our home with lots of laughter, energy and noise. Their little sister, April, came along a few years later, and her big brothers watched over her like guard dogs.

෨෨෨

Life continued, and as the years passed, we experienced the ups and downs of ministry. While our passion to help others know God never waned, the wounds we received in the process were sometimes more than we could bear. After facing the destruction of gossip, greed and selfishness in several churches, both Randy and I decided it was time to step away. Randy burned his books and sermons, and I decided I didn't want anything to do with ministry ever again. We found a church we enjoyed attending, but we believed our days of ministry had come to an end. Little did we know God had other plans.

When a small church asked Randy to step in as their interim pastor, I didn't want any part of it. Only 17 people remained active in the congregation. They'd been hurt, too. Randy began leading them in the truth of the Bible, and slowly God began mending their hearts. I, on the other hand, never wanted to fill the role of a pastor's wife again. I worked as a labor and delivery nurse, and thinking I could outsmart God, I purposely worked hours that prevented me from going to church. My feet began to ache with the long hours I spent working, but I ignored the pain. Sometimes the pain got so intense, Randy had to hold onto me to help me inside when I got home from work. I knew God must be trying to get my attention, but I refused to listen. My stubbornness convinced me that my way was best.

One day, I tripped over our puppy and fell onto the carpeted floor. When I tried to stand back up, I knew something was terribly wrong. Pain seared through my legs. An ambulance came, and the EMTs determined I had broken both of my femurs. Landing on a carpeted floor, I broke the two strongest bones in my body. The irony of it would have been funny, except for the excruciating pain. They couldn't get my IV in right, so they couldn't give me medication for the pain. I made the painful trek to the hospital, 30 miles away. They wheeled me into surgery, and my blood pressure spiked out of control. There on the operating table, the doctors didn't know what to do. My body started shutting down, and there seemed nothing they could do. By what must have been an act of God, I survived with both my legs, but my nursing career was over. The doctors told me that the bones in my body were basically mummy bones. Evidently, I'd been walking on broken bones for years. If God was trying to get my attention, he finally had it for good.

As I recovered in the hospital, I heard God's gentle voice wash over me once again.

Michele.

"Yes, Lord. I hear you."

You haven't been listening to me, my child.

"I know. I'm sorry. I'm listening now."

I've asked you several times to be a prayer warrior for me. Now will you do it?

"Yes!" my heart exclaimed.

❧❧❧

That small church of only 17 people grew to become New Hope Community Church, and Randy has been the pastor there since 1995. It is a place where people can come as they are and discover the God who made them and loves them. The people of this church are unlike any other I have ever known. They truly love each other and accept anyone who walks through the doors. God filled this church with hurting people, and he healed us and made us whole. We aren't perfect, but we want everyone who walks into our church to leave with one thing — hope.

I look back on my life, and my heart bursts with thankfulness. I'm even thankful for the difficulties. I walked through the fire of sorrow and disappointment. There were days when I felt that everything I ever hoped for was nothing more than a pile of ashes. But God raised me up out of the ashes and gave me a hope that cannot fade.

I see God's hand in every detail of my life. In the joy and the pain, he gently guided me to come toward him, drawing me ever closer to his heart.

The words of Micah 7:8 often come to my mind as I remember God's goodness. It reads, "Though I have fallen, I will rise. Though I sit in darkness, the Lord will be my light." I have indeed risen — out of the darkness and into the light of Christ.

VICIOUS CYCLES
THE STORY OF JETT
WRITTEN BY AMEERAH COLLINS

"Please don't think of this as just some court-ordered junk you're forced to endure, Jett. It's more than that. If you really want to improve your life, this is the place to do it."

The counselor sported a blue blazer and dark-rimmed glasses. She sat before me with her hands clasped on her large desk. She wore such an appealing mask: pursed lips and narrowed eyebrows full of concern. The quick tapping of her pen and glances at her watch gave her away, though.

I could practically feel thick waves of agitation rolling off her.

"You can say whatever you want, Cathy, but this place isn't for me." I chuckled sharply as I leaned toward her. "I'm not an alcoholic. I don't have a problem. I like to drink. That's it."

Alcoholics Anonymous. Counseling. Rehab. I've tried it all. It never works.

"Jett." Cathy sighed. "You may not believe you have an addiction issue right now, but one day you're going to realize how imprisoned you are by this habit. One day you're going to wake up and see how time has passed you by. And because of what? Alcohol? Drugs? A good time?"

Really, Cathy? What bull! This is a useless program. I can't wait to finish this crap.

I groaned and rubbed at my forehead. What a typical little speech. Cathy never altered her lines. Every day, every session, every doggone time I saw her, she offered the same old concept.

I checked my wristwatch. "Our time is almost up. No disrespect, Cathy, but this isn't for me. I know I've told you this a million times before, but these programs never work for me. For one, I know I'm not an addict. I don't have any problem that needs fixing. I just like to party."

"Then why can't you control your partying, Jett?" Cathy sighed and made a few harsh scribbles on her note pad. "Why the drunk driving? Why the accidents? Why the tickets?"

I stood from my seat, half contemplating her questions.

"Don't worry about me, Cathy. Believe me when I say that after my time here is up, you'll never see me again."

"I'm not sure if that's a good thing or a bad thing, Jett."

❧❧❧

Growing up, alcohol might as well have been an honored guest in my household. Liquor made its presence known at every large family function, simple gathering or typical nightly dinner. As just a young tyke, running around with training pants on, I remember watching the adults bounce with laughter around our living room, slinging their heads back with brown bottles attached to their lips. It felt great to be surrounded by family.

As my siblings and I grew a little older, my parents moved us all to an inner-city area of Michigan that promised a more prosperous life than we had. After we lived there for a few years, they decided to try something else, and we moved to the country. My dad worked on a farm every day and ran it on the weekends. Working with him taught my two brothers, two sisters and me the extreme importance and value of hard work.

Living in the country wasn't merely different because of the farm life, but also because, for a while, my father completely quit drinking. For those 10 years, Mom and Dad took us to church every Sunday and spent quality time with us on the farm. At the time, I didn't realize it, but our life was so wonderful because my father didn't drink. He had a clear focus on his work and family, but I didn't realize the change liquor could make in a person's life until I turned 13 years old.

"Sobriety ain't worth it." Dad slumped against the kitchen table, while Mom busied herself with the dishes. "I haven't gained anything from it. I might as well start drinking again."

"Really?" Mom turned to him with soap suds dripping from her fingers. "Ten years sober, and you haven't gained anything, Frank? Nothing at all?"

"Nope," Dad declared. He hopped up from his chair and began rummaging through the refrigerator and mumbling something about going on a beer run. Mom gazed down at the soapy water and shook her head.

When Dad started drinking again, trouble entered our

lives. Suddenly we stopped going to church, and Dad began staying out later than usual. He and Mom argued more often than they did before, and my siblings and I began to notice them drift apart. By the time I was 15 years old, it became apparent that they wouldn't last as long as Dad kept drinking. One evening, he pulled me into the living room while everyone else was out, either running errands, working the farm or hanging out.

"Jett." Dad rubbed his jean-clad knees. "I have to leave, son. I don't have a choice. Your mother and I are breaking up. I'm sorry, man."

With those simple words, I felt like he'd stomped on my heart and kicked it to the curb. I couldn't even gather my words as my chin began to tremble, and I harshly shook my head.

"No, no, you can't leave! How can you just up and leave like that? Is it because of Mom? Does she not love you anymore? Or, is it us? What did we do, Dad?"

Dad grabbed my shoulders. "Listen to me, Jett. Your mother and I busting up has absolutely nothing to do with you. It has nothing to do with your brothers and sisters, either." He huffed, and the smell of rank beer traveled from his mouth and up my nostrils.

"Then why? Why are you leaving?"

"This is what happens when you're an adult, son. Sometimes your marriage works out, and sometimes it doesn't."

"Please don't go." I continued shaking my head and angrily wiped at the tears streaming down my cheeks. "I don't care about all that adult crap. You can't leave. You have to stay and work it out. What are we supposed to do without you? You're my father!" I shouted. "Fathers don't leave their family, Dad!"

Dad briefly shut his eyes as my wails continued. He rubbed at his forehead and slowly stood to his feet. I grabbed his arm, but he swiftly turned, pulled me to my feet and held my hand in a fist against his chest. He eyed me, and with his eyes, he firmly told me to cease my cries.

"That's right," he said, nodding. "Just calm down. You'll be all right, Jett. I'm still your dad. I'll still be here for you. This is between your mother and I. You hear me?" He raised his brow and squeezed my fist when I didn't answer. "You got that, Jett? I'm leaving the house, not your life."

"Yeah," I hiccupped. "I got it."

Mom and Dad divorced, and two years later, Mom married Grayson. Honestly, I wanted to hate his guts simply because he wasn't my father. I blamed Grayson and even my mother for ruining my parents' marriage. When Mom and Grayson bought another house for our family, I refused to move in with them. Instead, I moved in with Dad.

Junior and senior year of high school proved to be a dream. I excelled academically and rose to the top of my class.

After school, I worked on a farm with my father, took care of my household responsibilities and made enough money to purchase my own car. Dad only had one rule:

When I returned home at night, the refrigerator needed to be stocked with beer.

That one simple rule was nothing for me to follow. However, that much freedom at such a young age eventually caught up with me. A few of my friends introduced me to marijuana. I not only enjoyed the mellowness and sense of serenity the high gave me, but I liked the popularity that came with it. Before long, I started dealing and became everyone's weed guy, and I loved it.

When I graduated from high school, I had a full scholarship to attend a prestigious university, and even though I took advantage of my freedom and smoked pot on a regular basis, I planned on going. However, months before my departure, my girlfriend got pregnant.

"Renee is a sweet girl, Jett, but please don't marry her. You two are too young for this," my father urged from across the kitchen table. "I know it seems like the honorable thing to do, but you don't have to marry Renee just because you got her pregnant."

I thumped my head against the wooden table and sighed. "Dad, we've been over this. It's the right thing to do. You and Mom raised me to be an honorable guy. I can't leave her out in the cold while I'm off in college doing my own thing. That's not right."

"You can't get your education, support your kid and work all at the same time. Giving up school and putting your future on hold is not an option, Jett. You need to think this through."

I threw my hands up. "I have, Dad! You think I'm ready to be a husband? You think I'm ready to suddenly walk into fatherhood? Believe me, I'm not. I just know what I have to do. I'm going to marry Renee, work on the farm, maybe start my own business someday and support my family as best as I can. It's what a real man would do — a grown man."

Dad shook his head. "Real man," he softly scoffed. "You're too young to be thinking like a real grown man. You're still a kid. What if I paid your child support, Jett? I want you to go to college. If you dedicate four years of your life, you'll be able to give Renee and your kid more than you can imagine. More than I ever gave you."

"Dad, I hear you. I really do." I reached out and gripped his shoulder. "But Renee is starting her senior year. It'll already be rough dealing with a pregnancy in high school. If I go off to college, it'll break her. I can't do that to her."

"Okay, son. Okay."

I married Renee, but my aspirations of being a great husband to her flew out the window once reality hit me in the face. She gave birth to our daughter Elena, and providing for them came so easy to me. However, being a devoted husband and father didn't. Slowly, I fell into a routine of working all day, drinking with the fellas in the evening and crashing at night.

I loved Renee, and I deemed Elena the greatest gift I'd ever receive, but I didn't cherish them the way a good husband and great father should have. I saw myself as a great provider to them, and I figured that was enough. Our bank account stayed rolling with money. Our refrigerator and cupboards remained shelved with food. Our closets and drawers were packed with clothing. My family didn't want for anything but my love.

I didn't realize that until it was too late, though.

During the first two years of our marriage, I became my father. During my later teenage years, I'd finally accepted that my parents' divorce occurred mainly due to my father's excessive drinking problem. Dad didn't give Mom the loving attention she deserved. He spent too much time downing beer and whiskey at the bar instead of returning home to his family. He appeared to value his work over his wife. Liquor had a tendency to turn Dad into a mean man.

Just like Mom couldn't live with a negligent alcoholic, Renee couldn't live with me.

After two years of marriage, we divorced.

ॐॐॐ

After the divorce, I felt so low. I didn't realize exactly what I'd lost until it slipped through my fingers. I'd let my high school sweetheart down. I no longer had the privilege of returning home to see Elena's cute, pudgy face. I knew I'd still get to see Elena, but I still felt like I'd lost them within seconds.

I needed something to pick me up and get me going again, so I joined the Army. Before I left for Basic

Training, I met Celine. I was 21 years old. She was a sweet girl I could see myself with long-term. Being with her made me appreciate my decision to join the Army more. I knew I would come back a more disciplined, structured and dedicated man for her.

During training, Celine found out she was pregnant with our child; however, she miscarried in the first trimester. The news didn't even reach me until days after she lost our child. A pit of gloom engulfed me, and it took everything within me not to go AWOL and rush home to her. I chose not to when she sent me a message saying, "Don't leave and get yourself in trouble." I felt helpless not being there for Celine. It took a while to forgive myself for that.

Although I desired to be a better man for Celine, my plans went askew. My stint in Basic Training reinforced the importance of hard work, taught me to be diligent in my career aspirations and lifted me from my depression. But I fell back into drinking and smoking marijuana. As I'd done with Renee, I stayed out till late at night and didn't cherish Celine.

Celine wasn't the sort of woman to question me, even after we got married. She may have asked where I was headed, where I'd been or what time I thought I'd be back, but she never pressed for many details of my life outside our home. If I told her lies about my whereabouts, she shrugged it off and let it be. I should have known I was hurting her, but I didn't.

I didn't change my ways after Celine gave birth to our

children, Jaxon and Jenna. And as they grew older, I still didn't change my ways. I worked hard and felt good about supplying the needs of my family, but I didn't spend quality time with them. I drank heavily, and when liquor got the best of me, I transformed into a cruel drunk with a sharp tongue. Whenever I stomped through the front door, everyone suddenly grew silent and began walking on eggshells.

"What do you mean, you don't get it?" I slammed my beer bottle onto the kitchen table and disregarded Jenna's hard flinch. I slid her worksheet closer to me and jabbed my finger at the problem. "It's simple multiplication facts. When you think about it, it's simple memorization. There is no difficult factoring involved. It's easy. Why aren't you getting it?"

"I don't know, Daddy." Her small voice trembled as her eyes focused on the pencil in her hand. "It's just hard. The sixes and the sevens aren't as easy as the fives."

"That's ridiculous, Jenna. You're probably the only student in your grade behind on your math. I was never like that as a kid. I was always at the top." I pushed the paper back to her and jumped up from my seat to grab another beer. I turned back and frowned as Celine hovered over Jenna whispering.

"The girl has to do it herself, Celine," I told her. "We've been over those multiplication facts with her a million times. If she hasn't got it by now, I don't know what to do with her."

Celine sighed as she rubbed Jenna's hair. "It takes a

little time — a little patience. That's all, sweetheart. You'll get it in time."

"Well, that's great, Celine. Go ahead and baby her. That works. Make me the bad guy."

"I'm not, Jett." She brushed past me and whispered, "You do that on your own just fine."

Through my liquor-induced fog, I couldn't wrap my head around how *my* children didn't catch on to academics as easily as I did. I usually learned a concept within minutes of the teacher introducing it. For years, I scolded all three of my children whenever they didn't excel as high or fast as I did in school.

ক্ষকক

By the time my kids reached high school, they feared the drunken me. Whenever Celine saw me stumble into the house, she knew it was time to either go into another room or brace herself for a verbal lashing. My drinking didn't subside over the years, it only grew worse. Since I worked so hard at my job, including the business I'd started, and ended my days at the bar, I was always so exhausted, and that irritated me.

The slightest things set me off. Although I never hit my wife or physically hurt my children, the harshness of my tongue cut their self-esteem, especially Celine's. I pained her so deeply that she just let my late nights and drunken stupors go. For years, I naively thought she wasn't the nagging sort of woman, but I later realized that she probably lacked the energy to push against my behavior. Maybe she deemed me a lost cause, until one night she decided to speak up when I was sober.

"I don't ask you much, but I want you to tell me the truth, Jett."

"About what, honey?"

"Are you seeing someone else?" She sighed when I didn't respond. I simply lowered my head. "I thought so. I'd heard a few things about you chasing women at those bars you frequent, and I've been watching you for a while."

"I'm sorry, Celine," I barely whispered. "God, I'm so sorry I did this to —"

"You're not the Jett I married." She slowly walked toward me and looked at me with tears in her eyes. "Nearly 20 years we've been together, but I can't do it anymore. I'm done."

I moved out of the house and bought a mobile home to stay in. I had my kids on the weekends, which caused me to limit my partying and drinking during their stays. Once again, I didn't know what I had until I lost it. For a whole year, I tried everything I could to get Celine back. I paid off her truck note, I paid off the house she lived in and I gave her a weekly stipend to ensure she lived life as financially comfortably as she had with me. Each time I called her to check in, pick up the kids or drop them off, I pled my case.

"I swear I'm going to change for you, Celine." I propped my shoulder against the house as we stood on her front porch and chatted. "I know our split-up was completely my fault. I cheated on you. I stayed out all night. I worked long hours and forgot about you. I —"

"I know what you did, Jett. You don't have to recount it all."

"I know." I palmed my forehead and sighed. "I just hate everything I did to you and the kids that hurt you guys. I never treated my family the way I was supposed to. I'm asking you to give me another chance to prove I can do better. I can be faithful, Celine. I can be a good father."

"I'm not ready, Jett. No."

Feeling like my life was crumbling and none of my efforts made it any better, I decided to take some time off work to get my head straight. I took $10,000 from my savings account, packed up my truck and headed south.

In Florida, I visited Elena in college and took her skydiving. I then made my way to Arizona to visit my mother and Grayson. While there, Grayson lifted me out of my funk.

"Jett." Grayson pulled a chair from under the kitchen table and sat beside me. "I've known for a while that you've been living a pretty wild life, and it's caught up to you. But I'm telling you right now, you're making everything too easy for that little wife of yours."

I straightened in my seat, "Huh? What are you talking about, Grayson? I'm just trying to mend all the damage I've caused to our marriage."

He snorted. "By making her life as comfortable or even more than when you were with her?"

"It's the right thing to do," I said, shrugging. "I neglected Celine for years, Grayson. We've been married almost 20 years, and a better part of those years have been hell for her."

Grayson nodded. "I understand, Jett. You've got a good heart. But enough is enough. You've apologized to Celine a thousand times over the course of a year. You've shown her that you love her, and she still won't budge on the separation. How many women in their right mind would jump back into a relationship with a man who's already making their life so sweet and easy? You paid off her car, house and you're giving her money, right?"

"Right."

"Well, that's it. Life is good for Celine. I wouldn't change anything if I was her, either."

"Hmm," I contemplated. "Do you think she's using me?"

"Not necessarily, Jett. I'm just saying you haven't given her a chance to miss you and actually think about giving you a second chance. Like I said, you've apologized and busted your butt for an entire year trying to win her back. It's time for her to make the next move."

"I think you're right, Grayson. I have been trying for a while, and I'm getting nowhere."

"Exactly." Grayson stood from his chair and patted my back. "It's time you draw the line, kid. Either get back together, or call it quits and start a new life. It's up to her."

I called Celine the next day, explained my thoughts, and she agreed to start over. I cut my road trip short and went straight back to my wife. As soon as I returned, we sat down, and after she said her piece and what she expected of our next go, I said mine. In the end, she agreed to never bring up my past mistakes again. We just wanted to move forward.

We stuck to that agreement. Even when we got into arguments or had our little spats here or there, Celine never threw my errors in my face. Although she kept up her end of the deal, I didn't stick to mine. Like an old wheel, I circled right on back into my mess. Drinking. Chasing women. Staying out late. Talking mean.

I messed up *again*, and she got rid of me for good.

❧❧❧

After Celine divorced me, I felt completely hopeless and ticked off at myself and drowned my misery in more alcohol and drugs. And not only marijuana this time. I picked up cocaine, and boy, did it take me for a ride. It didn't give me that "riding on cloud nine with the munchies" sort of high marijuana did. It didn't offer me the dizzying rage alcohol did. The euphoria of cocaine teleported me to another land. In my early 40s, I'd picked up one of the worst habits of all.

And I couldn't put the stuff down.

With my newfound habit and no one holding me accountable, I really began doing whatever I wanted to do. I lived my life on the edge. I got into three drunk driving accidents that should have killed me and could have killed someone else. The high speed and jolt of the impact propelled me through the windshield in one accident. In another, my car toppled over several times, and the crash actually tore a hole through the roof of my car. The third accident happened on a motorcycle. I was thrown 40 feet into the air and my helmet snapped off my head, yet I literally walked away with only a nasty bruise on the back of my leg.

My dumb decisions eventually led to me doing some time behind bars. A few times, the judge went easy on me and ordered me to attend Alcoholics Anonymous meetings, a couple rehabilitation centers or some type of counseling. I hated going to those places. I couldn't admit I had a problem with alcohol and drugs. I kept telling myself my so-called *habits* weren't actually *habits*, they were simple activities I enjoyed pursuing during my leisure time.

Nothing Cathy, the counselor, said ever got through to me. I considered the steps she wanted me to take toward sobriety as a joke. When she tried to speak to me about my future and improving my lifestyle, it entered one ear and exited out the other. Cathy seemed to hate that she could never break down my walls and trigger some kind of emotion in me that would get me to quit using. The last day of our counseling session, I told her she'd never see me again.

Months later I ate crow, and man, did it leave a sour taste in my mouth. I got into some trouble with the law and landed myself right back in Cathy's office. She didn't outright tell me, "I told you so," but I could practically read the smart-alecky remarks racing through her mind. Plus, her little smirk stood as a dead giveaway.

"Jett, you're back." Cathy propped her chin on her palm and eyed me.

"Let's just get this over with, Cathy. We know the drill." I rolled my eyes.

She softly chuckled and shook her head. "No can do, sir." Cathy popped up from her chair, strutted toward her office door and pulled it open. "I'm not your counselor this time. You're with Munroe this time, the owner of this center. He'll be better for you, Jett. Good luck."

Munroe didn't treat me like an addict like everyone else in those programs had. He treated me like a friend. Sometimes we talked in his office, other times we rode around in his Jaguar just talking about life. With Munroe, it seemed easier for me to admit my past mistakes, regrets, current dilemmas and insecurities.

I enjoyed Cathy's company, and I appreciated her trying to help me, but it was something about those man-to-man talks with Munroe that hit me.

"I've been watching you float in and out of here, Jett. Cathy is great, but she's not the counselor for you. She can't help, because she doesn't know you. I know you, Jett."

I huffed, amused. "How do you figure that?"

"Because once upon a time I was you." He flicked a glance at me. "I struggled with drugs and alcohol. I lost some of the best people to ever enter my life. I messed up, too, man. For a long time, I hated every stupid decision I ever made. I felt like I wasted so many years."

I nodded but didn't say anything. Munroe really did know me.

"Don't be ashamed of your past, Jett." Munroe turned down a busy street. "We can go around regretting our past for the rest of our lives. But here's the real fact. We wouldn't be who we are today, if we weren't who we were then."

Those conversations with Munroe stuck with me for years. I left his center, doing the same old thing, but I actually recognized my addiction for what it was. I still sniffed lines, smoked weed and got drunk after I left his facility, but I had to face the truth about myself.

A year or so later, my life hadn't gotten much better. My house burned down on my 45th birthday, and I had to move in with my mom and Grayson, who'd moved from Arizona and purchased a farm in Michigan near my own place.

Investigators deduced the fire started as a result of furnace complications, but I didn't see how that was likely. Honestly, I'm not sure if the furnace actually started the fire or if I left a lit cigarette burning.

I sat in my parents' home and asked myself, "What else can happen? It can't get worse than this. I'm an addict. My house is gone. I'm back home with my mom. My life is horrible."

I visited a friend of mine, who happened to be a pastor, and I talked to him about my issues. I sat in the office of his church and wept before him, laying all my problems out.

"I'm so tired, Don." I slumped over. "I don't know what else to do. I can't take any more of my life. I can't kick coke. I've lost two wives. My house burnt down, and for all I know, it could have been all my fault. I'm tired, man."

"Brother." Don walked over to my side of the desk, sat beside me and put his arm around my shaking shoulders. "I know you feel so exhausted and broken, but know that your situation is nothing God can't mend. He'll give you the strength to get through it, if you just ask him to."

"Well, I can't take any more, Don. I'm sick of my life," I cried. "If God will never put more on me than I can handle, then he's got to quit. This is too much."

"Well, I'll pray God doesn't give you any more, Jett. Life will get better. It has no choice but to."

After meeting with Don, I felt better about my future. Part of me truly wanted to live better and hang up the drugs and alcohol. I just didn't know how to quit it. I busied myself with rebuilding my house, and although I didn't go to church or really think much about God, I trusted that God would help me get my life back on track.

When I rebuilt my house, I built it as a duplex. My son Jaxon came to live with me, and I gave him the entire upstairs. He worked for me and became more of a business partner than another employee. Although many parts of my life did turn around, the cocaine and alcohol addiction remained.

During this time, I started dating Krissy. What made her so different from any other woman I dated was how our lifestyles easily aligned. She enjoyed heavy drinking. She smoked as much marijuana and sniffed as many lines of cocaine as I did. The amount of coke we did and how often we did it angered Jaxon. He never confronted me about it, though. He bottled his anger up.

"You didn't come into work today, Dad." Jaxon cornered me in the living room one night with his jaw clenched. "What happened to you?" He eyed me as I knelt beside the coffee table, trying to discreetly sweep away my powdery mess.

"I, uh, I had some unexpected errands to run." I straightened from my position and brushed past him into the kitchen. "How did everything go without me? Any complications?"

"Nope." Jaxon buried his fists in his pockets and rocked on his heels. "I took care of everything. While you were out running errands or whatever."

"Good." I glanced at him over my shoulder and watched him lower his head with a short shake. "I'll be there tomorrow, son. I don't have too much to do. I'll be there."

"Yeah. Okay, Dad." He turned from me and dragged his legs up the steps.

It didn't take long for Jaxon to quit my company and move out, then Krissy moved in. After a while, he'd become frustrated with my excuses for missing work and all the time Krissy and I spent doing drugs. Sometimes we even called off work, only to spend a week in the house getting high. We often discussed giving up drugs and alcohol for good, but each time we tried to live sober, one of us always slipped up.

"This has got to stop." Krissy cuddled next to me with our backs resting against the headboard. "Look at this," she half sobbed. She waved her hand at the empty bags with cocaine residue lying at our feet. "This is sick. *We are sick*, Jett. I wish we could just stop. I grew up in church. I know how my life is supposed to be. It shouldn't be like this."

I watched as Krissy roughly pushed the bags off the bed and onto the floor. Her shoulders vibrated as soft cries spilled from her mouth. I pulled her back toward me and held her.

"I know we need to quit, Krissy. I'm sick of the never-ending cycle, too." I spoke into her hair. "We've said this a hundred times before, but we seriously need to stop. We've been indoors for a whole week getting high. What kind of life is this? We're imprisoned by this crap."

"We can't bring home any more eight balls. We can't keep bringing ounces of coke into this house, Jett. If we stop, then we stop. Both of us. We can do this, but only together. No turning back this time."

"I know, honey. You're right. We can do this together. No turning back."

෨෨෨

When Krissy and I seriously decided to give up drugs and liquor, we did. We dealt with our withdrawal symptoms together and never gave in to the temptation to use. We worked hard to dig ourselves out of the financial hole we'd fallen into as a result of our expensive drug habit, and we even got married. Our only issue remained our complete boredom.

For so long, cocaine and alcohol ruled our life. It made us happy. We loved one another, but we were unhappy in our marriage.

The sober life proved to be very dull, mundane and rather routine. Something prominent was missing in our lives. We simply couldn't pinpoint what.

One day, Krissy approached me with some news from her doctor. She'd gone in for a mammogram, and the images revealed a cyst in her breast. Fortunately, the cyst was caught early, and Krissy's doctor removed it. The situation greatly bothered her, though.

"Jett." Krissy turned toward me in the passenger seat as I drove down I-94. "You know how I grew up in church, and my parents really instilled teachings of the Bible in me?"

"Yeah," I said, nodding. "What about it?"

"I've been thinking, and, um, if that cyst had the chance to grow into something much larger or detrimental to my health and I died, I would have gone to hell."

Puzzled, I glanced at her and slowed the truck down. She turned back in her seat, pressed her head against the headrest and let her eyes flutter shut. I understood every word Krissy said, but I couldn't understand why such a sweet, nonjudgmental, good person like her thought she could end up in hell. She didn't deserve eternal damnation — Krissy was a good person!

"No, you can't go to hell, Krissy." I shook my head in disbelief and pressed my foot onto the brakes. "You're the best person I know. If you're going to hell, I can't imagine how deep in hell I'll be. I've done much more horrible things than you."

"It's true, Jett." She looked at me. "If a person doesn't profess a firm belief in Jesus Christ, open his or her life and heart up to him and truly try to live by the teachings of the Bible, that person can't make it to heaven. It doesn't matter how sweet or nice you are. You have to believe and try your hardest to live a lifestyle that honors God."

I thought of Don and all the great conversations we had regarding the love of God and about changing my life. He never shoved his beliefs down my throat, but he always lent me an ear whenever I needed it. He always presented me with helpful words from the Bible to help me.

Don never forced me to believe as he believed, but his life sure intrigued me.

My mind drifted to a co-worker of mine, Drake, and how it was so obvious he possessed a great love for God. Drake treated everyone with such kindness, and he never let any negative situation or person get under his skin. Whenever presented with the opportunity, Drake spoke fondly of the Lord, almost as if he and God were friends.

How could he have that sort of connection with God? The great God? How?

I even thought of an old acquaintance from high school who ended up marrying my sister. Preston was such a rebellious teenager who constantly found his way on someone's bad list. However, I remembered how he gave his life to God in his early 20s and how completely different he seemed to be. My brother-in-law experienced a great change in his life.

I want that change. I need it.

An answer abruptly hit me. "We need to find a church, Krissy. Fast."

Our search for a church commenced that very day. We didn't care what denomination the church was, we sought a church that could tell us the truth about Jesus Christ. We wanted to join a church that didn't sugarcoat anything from the Bible — we wanted the God's-honest truth about our lives and how to make them better.

After we visited a few churches, a customer recommended my company to her pastor. While my guys and I did a job for New Hope Community Church, I noticed that the people I ran into were extremely pleasant and friendly. I didn't understand why they stopped me for conversation when I wasn't even a member.

When my team and I completed our work at the church and handed the pastor the bill, the church floored me once again. "Hang on a minute," he said. "I'll pay you now."

Wow, they didn't even ask for a discount, I thought.

Most churches I've worked with request a discount due to churches being a nonprofit organization. I guess they're not all the same.

I told Krissy one evening, "We should go to that church, honey. The one I did some work on. I don't even know what denomination they are, but those people were so nice. I mean, it's like you could see God shining through them."

"Seriously?" Krissy's eyes widened. "Whoa. That sounds like the kind of church we need, Jett. That's exactly how my church was as a child. Everyone just loved one another."

The following Sunday, Krissy and I visited New Hope Community Church. Once again, everyone greeted us with smiles and hugs. The uplifting songs, inspirational words and the way the people meshed so well with one another truly interested me. Even Pastor Randy reached me with his phenomenal message.

I learned it was never too late to give my life to God. There was absolutely nothing in my past that could stand in my way of developing a strong and true connection with Christ. All I needed, I realized, was a sorrowful heart for the negative deeds of my past and a sincere desire to be forgiven for my list of deepest regrets.

Learning such profound truths encouraged me to give my life to Christ. I asked God to enter my heart and wash away every wrongdoing of my past. My next step was baptism, a symbol of my new life in Jesus. When I was dunked under the water and lifted up, a heavy weight suddenly dropped off me. I felt so revived, new and light. It was like God washed away every bad thing I'd ever done. I believe he forgave me for everything. The drugs, alcohol, infidelity, lies and so much more. I felt like God just forgot all about that and took me in his arms, like a father would his reformed son.

❧❧❧

I decided to live my life for God by trying to be like his son, Jesus Christ. My hope is for others to know God as I've gotten to know him. I want people to see the significant change the Lord has made within me, especially the people who knew me during my worst days. I want my children to see me and say, "Look at Dad. He's a better man. God did that for him."

Just like my Christian friends never shoved their beliefs down my throat, I ask the Lord to help me when I speak to others about Christ — to give me the right words to say that will draw them to him, when they're ready. I want them to be in awe of God.

I learned the hard way that life isn't about chasing women or reaching the utmost high from drugs. Masking my misery with alcohol and partying didn't really take the pain away. Seeking satisfaction and recognition for my own benefit had no true reward.

For me, nothing else offered true joy, took away the pain or offered a lasting reward.

Nothing but God.

THE DAY THE WORLD STOPPED TURNING
THE STORY OF BETTY
WRITTEN BY SHARON KIRK CLIFTON

Someone knocked on my door.

Go away. Leave me alone. I'm waiting for a phone call, not a visitor.

Whoever it was knocked again, firmer this time.

With a heavy sigh, I went to answer it. Todd, my son-in-law, stood silhouetted against the late afternoon sun. He said nothing. He didn't have to. His knitted brows, firmly set mouth and clenched jaw told the story. He shook his head slowly.

The air left my lungs in a rush. "Nooooooooo," I moaned, stepping aside so he could come in. "Oh, Todd, no."

He slipped an arm around my shoulders and guided me to the sofa. "I'm so sorry, Mom. Leanne called just a few minutes ago."

"I knew it. I swear I knew it. I've felt he was gone for a few days now. Why didn't Leanne call me? I've been right here by the phone. Waiting."

His words were a whisper. "I think she thought it would be better if someone were with you when you found out."

As the dam holding back my tears broke, Todd reached for a tissue box and handed it to me.

I sat there sobbing, shaking and shivering.

I picked up a framed picture of him and looked into his eyes. "Oh, Lee. No. Not you, my sweet boy, my dear son."

Todd stood to leave. "I'm sorry, but I must get back to the girls."

I looked up at him.

"Did Leanne … did she say how …?"

"No. I don't think she would know that yet. She'll stop by when she gets back. Will you be okay?"

I think I nodded. That's what he expected me to do. But, no, I would never be okay again. I listened to the door latch behind him, leaving me alone with a heavy weight of sorrow.

❧❧❧

I was in my early teens when our family — my parents, my brother and we six sisters — moved to Orlando, Florida, from Michigan. Dad worked construction. Orlando experienced a growth spurt with the building of Disney World and all the businesses and neighborhoods springing up nearby.

I loved living in Florida. What girl wouldn't? We weren't too far from the ocean. We lived near that big, new amusement park they were putting up to honor a mouse in short pants. And there was no shortage of cute guys.

Ralph rode into my life on a brown Schwinn one warm

November day. He still sported his summer tan. His long, sun-streaked brown hair sailed back as he coasted down the street to the clicking of his 10-speed. A thin Amish-style beard framed his jaw line. He probably grew it just to prove he could.

I'd noticed him around the neighborhood before, usually riding his bike, but on that day, he stopped to talk. We discovered we had a couple things in common. We both liked rock and roll and smoking pot. A lot of pot. And he made me laugh, which is something I liked to do, even when it wasn't quite the appropriate response.

We'd known each other a couple of months when he asked me to marry him. I figured, why not? I was 16, and marriage could be my ticket out of the house, out from under my parents' thumb. I was six weeks shy of my 17th birthday when we married on St. Patrick's Day in 1972. It wasn't for love. I didn't know what real love was. We were hippie kids moving through life in a haze of marijuana smoke.

Ten months later, Lee was born.

I was ecstatic. That baby boy instantly won my heart. At last I had someone who would love me as much as I loved him. *Why couldn't Ralph be as happy with the birth of our baby as I was?* He was more enamored with his music and drugs than he was with Lee or me. At least, it seemed that way. I guess he liked him okay, but Lee was my little buddy.

We lived in a rented block house back in an orange grove. It was originally intended for migrant workers. I hated it. When we walked in at night and turned on the lights, palm-sized banana spiders scurried everywhere. I was afraid for Lee's sake. I'd get up in the middle of the night and go check to be sure he was okay. Fortunately, I never found a spider in his crib.

My pot smoking did nothing to lower my level of apprehension. Instead, it sent my mind crawling through myriad scenarios involving spiders. One night, I awoke in the closet, curled into a fetal position. I'd dreamt of the spiders and, in my sleep, had gone to the closet for safety. How I wished we could move from there, especially as Lee grew and spent more time playing on the floor.

Our little guy ran before he could walk. It took him a while to slow down to a walk. That's what got him in trouble with his daddy. Ralph had purchased an expensive new stereo system — one we really couldn't afford. When Lee took off at full speed across the floor, he made the stereo needle skip on the records, often scratching them.

"Bett, can't you keep this kid from running?" Ralph took a record from the stereo and held it up in front of my face. "Look at that."

"I'm looking. I can't help but look. What am I supposed to see?"

"That scratch! Didn't you hear the Beatles singing, 'Let it be, it be, it be, it be?' I swear, that kid's gonna ruin all my tunes."

"He's a baby, honey. A toddler. They run."

"Yeah? Well, he's gonna be a baby with a beat butt, if he don't stop it."

True to his word, Ralph started grabbing Lee as he ran by and swatting his bottom. Despite my efforts to keep Lee out of the room when Ralph was playing his music, that little fellow would manage to sneak right back. He wanted to be with his daddy, an impulse that came as natural as running.

Maybe I overreacted, but I felt Ralph was abusing Lee and that it was my responsibility to protect my little boy, to get him out of there so he could be a normal kid. In 1974, I divorced Ralph. It wasn't easy because I had come to love Lee's daddy. Not the crazy, head-over-heels, drop-dead kind of love, but love, nonetheless. I didn't want to leave him, but I worried that the spankings would get harder as Lee grew. After the divorce, though, I didn't think I'd ever stop crying.

For a while, I waited tables, but that didn't work out. My mom was willing to care for Lee, but he'd have none of it. He cried incessantly. So I quit my job and went on welfare to be with him.

My life was a mess. I was smoking weed, drinking, partying and sleeping around. I had gotten another job by that time, but I don't recall where I worked. Too many brain cells burned up from the drugs and booze, I guess. When I became pregnant, I told a woman I knew, Delilah, who was a nurse. We weren't actually friends, but she and I liked to drink beer and shoot pool together. She was always getting pregnant by her various boyfriends, pregnancies that ended in abortions. For her, termination was a form of birth control, nothing more.

"So, hon, are you in your first trimester?" she asked.

I nodded, not really sure when my last cycle was.

She patted my arm. "No problem. Get an abortion. Everybody's doing it these days."

I called a women's clinic in the Orlando area. The receptionist set up an appointment for what she called a counseling session.

The day of the appointment, I kept telling myself it was okay. After all, I had no idea who the father was. I already was a single mom trying to make ends meet. Another child would be a financial burden and an inconvenience. It wasn't right to bring a baby into the world under those circumstances, was it? And, as Delilah said, everybody was doing it. How many abortions did she say she'd had?

When the intake nurse heard my story, she nodded sympathetically. I let her convince me that in the first trimester, my baby was actually a mere blob, a mass of cells. In my heart, I didn't believe that was true.

My sweet Lee was waiting for me at home. I knew he hadn't started out as a blob that turned into a human baby the instant he was born. He was a baby from the very beginning. Besides, I wasn't sure I was within the limits of the first trimester.

As they prepped me for the procedure, I thought about Lee. I could smell his freshly shampooed hair, feel his gentle kisses on my cheek. The abortion began. I could hear Lee's giggles as I tickled his toes. Stainless steel clanged against stainless steel.

The nurse wiped my eyes with a tissue. "It'll be over in just a moment. You'll be all right."

No, I wouldn't.

"Oh, my God." The abortionist's voice sliced through my thoughts and jerked me back to the present reality. "We shouldn't have done this. She's too far along." His eyes glared at me over his surgical mask.

A great wave of remorse washed over me.

❧ ❧ ❧

That would have been a great time to turn my life around. After all, I truly did regret the abortion. But I guess not enough. I continued my partying ways and became pregnant again. Although it felt selfish, I allowed myself to get a second abortion.

Shortly after that, I met Duke. His rugged good looks attracted me, that and the fact that he liked to party as much as I did. Duke lived deep in the backwoods near Orlando. While I never moved in with him, he did father the child of my fourth pregnancy, one that ended in a miscarriage. Duke never knew about the child.

Mixed emotions filled my heart at this loss. Part of me grieved at the loss of another child, but another part felt rescued because I had no further ties to Duke. I never felt quite safe with him. I felt this gave me a chance to just stop seeing him.

Next to come along was Joe, a real charmer. He had a way of making a woman feel loved, and I needed that. By the time Joe came into my life, I was pretty down on myself. I carried the burden of knowing I'd committed two abortions, suffered a miscarriage and had so many sexual trysts I couldn't even count them. A neighbor introduced me to Joe, and we hit it off right away.

While I was expecting my daughter, I discovered I wasn't the only woman Joe charmed. Any girl who showed him some affection was fair game where he was concerned. I had thought he was different, but when I learned he wasn't, I told him to leave. I wasn't willing to share him. We continued to be friends.

Shortly after we parted ways, he began seeing a younger girl and talked her into living with him back near Okeechobee Swamp. They both were found dead with bullet wounds to the back of their heads, execution style. The police declared it a cocaine deal gone bad. Upon reading that in the newspaper, all I could think was, *That could have been Lee and me!*

Someone was watching over us.

෩෩෩෩

At just after 4 a.m. on July 10, 1976, I awoke to a lot of cramping in my belly. The night before, I had gone to a friend's house, where I drank a bottle of castor oil and took a two-mile walk. The castor oil was wreaking havoc in my gut, so I hurried to the bathroom. The oil did its job, and I realized I was in labor.

I called my ex-mother-in-law.

"Myra, the baby's coming. Now!"

"Oh! Okay. Hang on, sweetie. I'll be right there."

I was living in my parents' house at the time. They had moved, so I rented from them. One of my sisters was staying with me to watch Lee when I went to the hospital.

When Myra got there, she grabbed my suitcase. "How close are the contractions?"

"About two minutes apart."

"Oh, have mercy! We've got to hit the road running. Let's go!"

I was miserable on that ride. I could hardly sit and had to prop myself up.

"Hon, there's no way I can get you to the hospital in time. I'm dropping you off at the fire station. They can make it a whole lot faster. And they're trained to deliver in emergencies. We'll meet you there."

I just nodded, trying not to have the baby in her car, a Volkswagen bug. Her two daughters were in the backseat.

At the fire station, Myra had to awaken the firemen. They got me into the rescue truck.

"Now, ma'am," one of the firemen said, "if your water breaks, you be sure to let us know. We'll have to stop, because they want us to deliver the baby right then, so you won't have a dry birth."

It broke.

"Excuse me, gentlemen. Uh, my water just broke."

"Are you sure?"

"Pretty sure. How many babies have you guys delivered?"

"None, ma'am. But we've been trained. We know what to do."

"How far are we from the hospital?" I was hoping they could make it.

"About two blocks away. We have to stop and deliver the baby here."

Three men were in the unit. The driver stayed at the wheel, ready to take off as soon as the baby came. One man sat at my head, offering me his hand to squeeze. I think I probably broke every bone in his hand. The third was the designated deliverer. He was in position to catch the baby, but both rear doors of the unit were wide open. One of the other two told man #3 to close the doors to prevent rubbernecking drivers from wrecking as they tried to see what was going on. At that point, my crazy sense of humor kicked in, and I started laughing. That got them to laughing, too. It relieved some of the tension.

After Leanne was born, we went on to the hospital. All three firemen asked for coffee when they walked in.

A nurse met them with a smile and thrust a clipboard into one set of hands. "No coffee until the paperwork is done."

❧❧❧

The mantra of my generation was "Don't trust anyone over 30." In 1983, I hadn't yet reached 30, but Burt had. In fact, Burt was nearly 70 when I met him at the seafood restaurant where I worked. He wasn't bad-looking for an old man, and he was nice.

His wife had left him — I figured she knew he stepped out on her — so he liked to come eat lunch at a time when we weren't too busy, when he might get a little more attention from the waitresses.

One day, he came in about a half hour after the lunch crowd had cleared. Catching my eye, he gestured to a corner table. "Hey, honey, this one of yours?" He liked to sit in my section whenever possible.

"Look around, Burt. You're the only customer in here. The other girl's on her break. You own the place right now. Sit wherever you please. What can I get for you?"

"You."

"Pardon?"

"I'll take you."

"Now, Burt, the only thing fresh here is the food. Let's keep it that way."

He snorted. "Guess I'll settle for the usual."

"Steamed shrimp over ice."

"You know me so well. Will you peel them for me?"

"Don't I always?"

A few minutes later, I returned with his order.

He patted the chair next to him. "Sit."

"You're going to get me fired."

"No, I won't. I'm friends with your boss. I want to ask you something."

I scooted onto the chair and picked up a shrimp to de-shell. "Shoot."

"I've got a birthday coming up. How about you helping me celebrate?"

I held the shrimp out to him, and he took it with his teeth. "I don't date married men."

"Married! Psh! She went crying home to her mama. You call that married?"

"Are you divorced?"

"Not exactly."

"Then you're married. Here, have another shrimp." I poked it in his mouth. "Here comes another customer. You're on your own, big boy."

❧❧❧❧

I didn't see Burt for a couple weeks. When he finally returned, he told me he just got back from the Bahamas. He also made sure I knew he'd taken some sweet young thing with him.

He continued to ask me out until I finally gave in. When he found out I smoked weed, he told me he could get me the best I'd ever smoked. He smoked a pipe, but not pot. Nonetheless, he kept me supplied. Once, I called him my sugar daddy. That infuriated him.

"Never call me that again."

"I'm sorry," I said. "Man, I was just teasing."

"That's the same thing as a dirty old man. And I'm *not* that!"

❧❧❧❧

When my sister Hope and her husband, Paul, moved from Texas to Florida to find work, they stayed with Lee, Leanne and me. My life began to turn a corner.

Hope, my "wild child" sister, had changed from party girl to holy roller. First thing she did when they landed on my doorstep was go looking for a church, as if that was the most important thing on her to-do list. She found one and asked me and the kids to go with them.

"I don't think so, Hope," I said. "We're not exactly churchy type people."

"Well, what about the kids? Can they go?"

"I guess, if they want to." Lee said no, but Leanne was eager to go. She started attending regularly.

Then one day Hope told me Leanne had asked Jesus to be her Savior and wanted to get baptized. Okay. Now, my sister was speaking another language, one I didn't know.

"Jesus? Savior? Baptized? What does that all mean?"

Hope smiled, not a smirk, but a genuine smile that reached her eyes. "I'm glad you asked, big sis. Do I smell coffee?"

"Yep. I just made a fresh pot."

"Good. Let's go talk." Leanne followed us into the kitchen. I poured our coffee, Leanne got herself some chocolate milk and we all sat around the table.

I blew on the surface of my coffee before taking a sip. "Okay. What's this all about?"

Hope launched into an incredible tale about a God who had created a beautiful, perfect world, who had formed man and woman with his own hands and breathed into them his own breath. She told of how sin came into the world and brought with it pain, suffering and death.

"And just what is sin?" I asked.

"God is perfectly good, clean and holy. Sin is whatever keeps us from being as perfect as God is. Sin is the wrong things we do."

I threw my hands up in the air. "Then I'm a goner, for sure, Hope, because I'm far from perfect."

"That's the point, Bett. We all are goners, sinners. That's where Jesus comes in. The Bible tells of how Jesus, God's only son, came to the earth he created to live a sinless life, die a horrible death on the cross to pay the debt for our sin and —"

"Aunt Hope, can I tell?" Leanne didn't wait for permission. "They put his dead body in a tomb — kinda like a cave — and after three days he came back alive."

Hope chuckled. "Right on, kiddo!"

I took a deep gulp of my coffee and wiped my hand across my mouth. "Okay, I get all that, but what's baptism all about?"

"If you're —"

"Let Leanne tell me, since she's the one who wants to get baptized."

Leanne straightened up in her chair and folded her hands, resting them on the table. "Well." She drew the word out. "When Jesus calls us to follow him, and we're really, really, *really* sorry for our sin and we say yes, we want to follow him, then we walk into water with the preacher, and he says some Bible verses or something and leans us baaaaaack in the water and *pulls* us up real fast. That lets people know we really, really, really meant it when we said we wanted to follow Jesus. And, Momma, I do really, really, really mean it. Will you come see me get baptized? I'm going to pinch my nose hard so I don't drown."

"Yes, sweetheart. A herd of wild horses couldn't keep me away."

I went, but I was stoned out of my head, a situation that didn't help my perception of the service. The people were very lively, clapping and singing. Many of the women wore their long hair in elaborate dos that required metal reinforcement to hold it in place. As they became more active in their style of worship, I watched bobby pins flying in every direction.

Then came time for Leanne's baptism. My mind was fuzzy, my vision blurry, as I tried hard to focus. My dear daughter walked slowly into the water that reached to her underarms. She gave a little shiver and turned to look out over the congregation. She found me quickly and smiled. I think I nodded and returned her smile. I have no idea what the preacher said. I just remember watching him lean her back into the water until she was completely immersed and raising her up with a *whoosh*. Water sheeted from her face and hair as she rubbed her eyes and smiled. All the people began singing the chorus of a song.

As strange as that little church seemed to me that first time I attended, I liked it, and I liked the people, so much so, in fact, that I began going regularly. The more I learned about Jesus, the more I wanted to know. Finally, one Sunday when the pastor invited people to come forward and accept Jesus' invitation to follow him, I went. In Leanne's words, I was really, really, *really* sorry for my sin.

As I knelt at that wooden altar, my mind raced over the long list of my transgressions, a list that included promiscuity, abortions and addictions to drugs and alcohol. How could Jesus forgive all of that? Yet, I believed he could. I'd read in the Bible that if we confess our sins, he is faithful and true and will forgive us of our sins and wash them away, clean us up, so that when God looks at us, all he can see is the holy perfection of his only much-loved son, Jesus.

Now, I had to have a little talk with Burt.

৯৬৯৬৯৬

"Burt, I am now a follower of Jesus Christ."

"That's fine. Everyone has a right to his or her own religion."

"It's not a religion. I have a relationship with Christ, a close friendship. That means I will no longer engage in sex outside of marriage."

I decided that the best thing I could do was to leave the area for a while, to put some distance between Burt and me, so the children and I went to visit some family members. While we were away, Burt's estranged wife died. When we returned, Burt asked me to be his wife, and I said yes. On May 16, 1986, Burt, I and the children drove to Valdosta, Georgia, where Burt and I were married before a judge.

Two and a half years later, on August 24, 1988, Burt died of a heart attack. In the wake of his death, I slid away from God, committing afresh many of the sins I had repented of when I began my journey with Jesus.

Some of Lee's friends were doing drugs, and they brought me cocaine. Though I resumed smoking marijuana, coke became my drug of choice. I also started smoking cigarettes. I continued going to church and helping out in the nursery. One day I was cleaning the church when the pastor noticed the smell of the cigarettes that clung to my clothing and hair.

"Betty, do you smoke?"

I admitted that I did.

"Oh, I'm sorry, but one of our nursery guidelines states that smokers cannot work with the little ones. It's not good for them to be around secondhand smoke."

After that, I stopped going to church. I sank deeper into my old ways. I wasn't upset with the pastor, the people or even the rules. I knew smoking wasn't good for me.

Leanne hated the person I had become. So did I.

❧❧❧

In mid-1991, Leanne told me she was pregnant. She was 15. I knew the boy responsible and didn't want to stay in the area where he could continue to influence her, so we moved to Michigan. My parents were there, and they said we could stay with them for a while.

When I suggested that Leanne get an abortion, she was adamant.

"Absolutely not, Mom! How can you even suggest such a thing? What I'm carrying is a baby! A human baby. And he or she is not responsible for what I did."

I hadn't told her about my own history, and I figured that wasn't the time to disclose it. Knowing what I went through, remembering the horrible load of guilt I carried around because of what I'd done, I couldn't believe I'd suggested that to my little girl. *God, please forgive me,* I prayed, and I begged my daughter to forgive me, too.

Leanne enrolled in school once we got to Michigan. Because she was pregnant, she had to attend an alternative school. That was where she met Todd. They started dating and soon moved in together. After her first child — a daughter — was born, they had three more girls before deciding to marry. Leanne recommitted herself to living for Christ. She told me that above everything else, she wanted her children to grow up in a Christian home. Her love for Christ put me to shame.

∾∾∾

My sister Lynn worked at a local bar, and I liked to go in, drink beer and shoot pool. Eventually, I got a job there, too, so when business was slow, I played. With all that practice, I got pretty good.

That's how I met Jim. He came in all the time. The first thing I noticed about Jim was his eyes. He had the most incredible sparkling blue eyes. I had seen pictures of the Caribbean. That was the color. They shone even in the dim lighting around the bar.

He was a farmer, and I liked to listen to him tell about how he handled his livestock. He was kind to his animals.

Jim was different from any man I'd ever known. He didn't smoke, drink or do drugs. At the bar, he'd order a Coke.

We spent a lot of time talking and playing pool. Finally, he suggested I move in with him. I did.

My parents' opinions of Jim were polar opposites. My dad loved him.

"Now there's a man's man," he said once. "A farmer who isn't afraid to work hard and get dirty. He seems to be careful with his money, too." *He pinches pennies until they squeal, Dad.* "And he's taking care of my girl."

The main reason Mom didn't like him, though, was that he never said he loved me. Never.

While I was with Jim, I underwent surgery for cervical cancer and endured subsequent radiation treatments. I also had two heart attacks. I didn't know about the first one until I suffered the second one.

I didn't go to church while I lived with Jim, but he knew I said I was a Christian. He once asked me about it.

"So what does your God think about our living arrangement?"

"He doesn't like it, of course. It's wrong. Obviously,

141

you realize that, or you wouldn't ask the question. But he'll forgive me when I ask."

"Just like that, he'll forgive you?"

"Yes."

How could I say such a thing? Sure, I believed God would forgive me if I truly was sorry, but I knew it wasn't right to keep doing the same sin over and over, like a dog returning to its vomit, with the intention of asking forgiveness. I felt pretty sure that was an abuse of his grace, his unmerited favor. Our sin cost Jesus everything. We shouldn't take his sacrifice lightly. And I was doing exactly that. I was sick at the thought.

As Easter Sunday 2002 approached, I asked Mom if she'd be interested in going to New Hope Community Church with me. She said yes, she'd been wanting to go. She knew Pastor Randy Royston, his wife, Michele, and Michele's mother.

When we walked in the doors and into the sanctuary, the people made us feel welcome, as though we'd been attending for years. Mom was glad to see Pastor Randy again, but we were disappointed that we didn't get to see Michele, who was home sick.

That Easter Sunday morning, when Pastor Royston gave the invitation for anyone to come pray at the altar, I went up. I asked Jesus to forgive me for walking away from him those last few years. I knew I had dishonored him with my life in allowing myself to slip back into the muck and mire of my life before Christ. I prayed that he'd help me live as he wanted me to.

Mom also went to the altar that morning, and she became a Christ-follower. When God accepts a sinner and forgives that person, that's what you'd call a miracle — something contrary to human understanding — but God worked another miracle in my momma's life. She, who had been an alcoholic for 40 years, lost all desire for alcohol that Easter Sunday morning at the altar of New Hope Community Church.

When I told Jim that, as a woman of God, I had to move out, it didn't faze him. That stabbed at my heart. I'd been with him for nine years. We'd gone through a lot together. We got along well. We never fought or had harsh words. Yet, he didn't seem affected at all by my leaving. For nearly a decade, he obviously considered me little more than a maid and a sex toy.

As God would have it, Pastor Randy's mother-in-law had a basement apartment for rent that I could move right into. I didn't feel I deserved God's consideration, but it looked like he'd already made a place for me.

తతత

The year 2003 was one of the worst in the lives of our family because we suffered so many losses.

In January, an uncle died. Then, my sister Lynn, who had been diagnosed with a brain tumor and had undergone surgery and radiation that November, refused chemotherapy. When she was dying, the people of New Hope Community Church stepped up to help us through that time. Mom went every day to stay with Lynn until her husband got home from work, so the church people prepared meals and took them to Dad. Lynn came to Christ before she passed on March 30. Therefore, we reassured ourselves that we could be certain we'll see her again in heaven.

In July, two other uncles died. My niece was killed in a car wreck in September, and an aunt died in November.

When December 31 slipped into history, I thought surely I had endured the worst year of my life.

But I was wrong.

༒༒༒

In 2005, I managed the branch office of a cash advance company. I hated that job. I felt like a mafia loan shark. In fact, Dad called me Guido. I'd been doing it for six years and was ready to move on to something else. All I needed was a little nudge to get out of there.

That nudge came one Friday afternoon, as I and another employee were closing up. I was working at my desk when someone entered, and I heard my colleague say, "How can I help you?" Something about the way she said it sounded strange, so I looked up to see what was going on. A woman stood at the counter with a scarf covering the bottom half of her face. All I could see were her eyes, but something about them was familiar. She must have recognized me, too, because she tugged the scarf up a little higher until it brushed her lower eyelashes. *Too late, chick!*

She tossed a bag at my colleague and said, "Put all the money in there." She laid a gun down on the counter. It looked like a BB gun to me.

"Is this for real?" I said.

Our company had certain procedures that we were supposed to follow, but our branch didn't follow them to the letter. We did things in a way that worked best for us. So my colleague emptied the cash from her drawer into the bag, but there was another drawer that held about $6,000. The robber thought she had all the money, so she ordered us to lie down on the floor.

We both did as she said. I started praying out loud, calling out to Jesus. The other clerk, who also went to New Hope, started praying aloud, too.

We must have freaked the robber out. "Oh, would you people shut up?" She yelled it. "I'm not going to shoot you. Now, lay there, and count to a hundred. Don't get up till you're done. Hear?"

We listened for the door to close behind her, and then we jumped up. I didn't even know I could do that anymore. I must have had springs on my butt! I hurried to the security buttons, pushing the one that indicated a robbery in progress. The security company notified the police who came right away. They sent a portion of the video from our surveillance camera to local TV stations. The manager of another branch of our company recognized the robber from her walk, and the police arrested her. She had worked at another branch, so I'd apparently met her at a regional meeting at some point.

She had hit two other branches, trying to get money for a restaurant she wanted to open.

I couldn't go back to work there after that, so I quit my job. That was a bad day.

But not the worst.

❧❧❧

February 16, 2010, was the day my world stopped turning.

Dad's 80th birthday was nearing. I was trying to get all the loose ends of a big celebration tied up, helping Mom with the last-minute details. I'd been trying all week to get hold of Lee, who lived in a nearby town. He didn't answer when I called, and he didn't respond to the messages I left on his answering machine. I called Leanne to see if she'd talked with him.

"No, Mom, but you know he's been having trouble with his phone. He knows about the celebration, right?"

"Yes, but I just don't feel good about this."

"Tell you what. To ease your mind, Erin and I will run over to his place and make sure he remembers about the get-together." Erin was my granddaughter, Leanne's oldest. "I'll call you from there, either from his phone or, if it's not working, from a pay phone."

"Thanks, hon. I appreciate that."

"Not a problem. Love you."

"Me, too, you. Be careful, sunshine."

I tried to keep myself busy until a reasonable time had

passed. After a couple hours, I stopped pretending to be busy and planted myself by the phone. Another hour passed. Still no word.

Someone knocked on my door.

Go away. Leave me alone. I'm waiting for a phone call, not a visitor.

Whoever it was knocked again, firmer this time.

With a heavy sigh, I went to answer it and saw Todd, my son-in-law. He said nothing. He didn't have to.

The air left my lungs in a rush. "Noooooooooo," I moaned.

❦❦❦

Leanne came by later that evening. It was past my usual bedtime, but I wouldn't be doing any sleeping that night, maybe never again.

For about a half hour, we just held each other and cried. When she finally could talk, it was barely above a whisper.

"I had Erin wait in the car, in case he wasn't dressed or something. I knocked on the door. There was no answer. I was glad he had thought to give me a key to his apartment. I unlocked the door and opened it slowly. I could … I called his name, but there was no answer. By that time, I knew there wouldn't be. I found him leaning up against the bathroom wall. Apparently, he had been sick and gone in there. Mom, listen. This is so hard to say, but … he didn't *just* pass."

"What do you mean?"

"He … that is … he's been gone for a few days. I don't think it would be wise for you to see him."

I heard a mournful wail that seemed to erupt from the earth's core, then realized it was me. My son, my only son!

You know, don't you, God? You watched your son, your only son, die for me, for the world's sin. You alone understand.

We received the coroner's report a few days later.

Lee died of pancreatitis about two weeks before Leanne discovered his body.

Leanne and her girls worried about me. Following Lee's death, I became a hermit, refusing to do anything or go anywhere. I canceled cable and Internet. I seldom answered the phone. I really didn't care whether I lived or died. My joy had been stolen.

One day, Leanne approached me about my emotional state.

"Mom, you wouldn't hurt yourself, would you?" Tears rimmed her eyes as she asked the question.

For a moment, I went quiet, thinking. *Would I? I wanted to.*

"No, darling. I promise. I won't hurt myself. That would hurt you. And those sweet girls. And Mom. But I wouldn't get mad at God if he decided to call me home."

Then on May 20, he called my mom home instead.

No contest. The year 2010 was the worst of my life.

When I allowed him to, Jesus gave me his peace. I read in the Bible where he promises never to leave us or forsake us. I also read Isaiah 41:10: "Do not fear, for I am with you; do not anxiously look about you, for I am your God. I will strengthen you, surely I will help you, surely I will uphold you with my righteous right hand."

Many times, as I crawled through my own valley of grief, God used the people of New Hope to remind me of his love. They were his messengers, willing to weep with me, pray with me, rejoice with me at the birth of my first great-grandchild and sometimes just listen to me.

On Father's Day of 2014, I thought I was having a third heart attack. Sharp pains radiated through my chest. I went to the ER. It wasn't a heart attack, but I believe God let me suffer that to make me realize I did want to live. I still had much to live for. If I ever doubted it, I needed to look no further than the face of my little great-grandbaby.

Jesus resurrected my joy.

Did I still mourn Lee's passing? Of course. But at last the world began to turn on its axis again. Like a person going through physical therapy, I had to relearn how to laugh. Daily I drew on God's strength to rejoin the land of the living. I got active at New Hope, serving wherever I could.

If anyone asked me whether I thought his or her sin burden was too dark, too much for God to forgive, I would reply from personal experience that as long as you have breath, you are never beyond the reach of God's forgiveness through Jesus Christ.

DEATH, DOUBT AND DIVORCE
THE STORY OF JAMES
WRITTEN BY ADAM KNECHTEL

The verdict was in.

The judge, a prominent figure, tall and robust, stood with his hands silently perched upon his podium. He looked inexplicably powerful and relaxed, almost as if the podium was actually reaching up to him for support, rather than he resting on it for stability. He began to speak and though I listened intently, his words blurred together in my mind. This much I knew: The verdict was in, and I had lost.

How could this happen? After everything I've been through, after everything she has done, how could they possibly side with her? Why is this allowed to happen?

Thoughts smashed into one another in my mind, as if a tumultuous sea plunged me further away from the hope of ever again feeling solid ground. I packed what few belongings I owned and headed home to Michigan.

છે છે છે

I was born and raised in Michigan. My parents' marriage had seen better days, and they divorced before my 5th birthday. I stayed with my mother and sister in Michigan, while my father disappeared from my life entirely.

Every Sunday morning brought the same routine: Mom would push a Bible at me and force me to attend church services with her. As a result, I attended church regularly and was baptized into the Christian faith at the age of 13. However, her incessant prodding eventually turned me away from my faith, instead of deeper into it like she desired.

The one thing I enjoyed less than religion was school. I never put forth any effort greater than what was required to produce a passing grade.

That, coupled with my ever-increasing desire to get away from home, drove me to enlist in the United States Air Force.

And so, I spent my 21st birthday reporting for Basic Training in the grand ole State of Texas. Within a year and a half, I was stationed in North Carolina at Seymour Johnson Air Force Base as a "grease monkey" of sorts, working as crew chief on the F-15 Strike Eagles.

When I arrived in North Carolina, I visited a few local churches, but they all failed to rekindle any desire or passion for my long-dormant faith, and as time passed, I gave up the pursuit entirely.

I met Ava within a few months of arriving in North Carolina. In the middle of a downtown karaoke bar, we immediately hit it off. After dating for a couple of years, I popped the question, she said yes and we tied the knot in 2008.

Nearly a year later we sat together in the doctor's office, nervous, excited and patiently awaiting the news. I paced the floor feverishly. Ava leaned back, calm and collected as our doctor began the ultrasound.

After a few minutes of grainy black-and-white images and constant reassurances of health and development, our doctor paused his work and looked up at us.

"Well," he began. "It's a girl!"

There was brief silence followed by sudden eruption.

"It's a girl! We're having a girl!"

Shortly thereafter, in March of 2009, we welcomed our daughter Paige into the world. She had bright blond hair, like I once had as a child, and her dark brown eyes, which were hidden behind high cheekbones, were saturated with unconditional, childlike love. When I looked into those beautiful, innocent eyes and playfully poked a finger at her belly, she would stare right back and with minuscule fingers wrap her hands around mine with the utmost delicacy and tranquility. Every moment, pure ecstasy.

But in August of that same year, I also received my first deployment orders for immediate departure to Afghanistan.

You can't be serious! My girl's barely 5 months old, and I am already forced to leave her? Barely 5 months old and I'm already being pulled away? How can this be happening?

I simply could not understand. Thoughts, curses, ruthless threats, desperate pleadings and anguished petitions spewed forth from my mind, directed at and received by no one in particular.

While my daughter grows up at home with my wife, I

will be withering away in some godforsaken desert, grumbling about my loneliness and despair with an entire host of begrudging, lonely men.

Those last few precious days with my wife and daughter were as satisfying as they were haunting. I clung to my daughter as if time had no influence over me, as if the longer I held her in my arms, the longer I would be allowed to stay.

And then I left.

I arrived in Afghanistan in late August on a painfully dark night. A dark so deep and heavy that it seemed to seep down from the sky and slouch upon the earth beneath. As if the night air clung to its surroundings, desperately hoping to pull itself away from the coming day.

Boom!

The first mortar round went off somewhere nearby, followed by the furious shuffle of hands and feet preparing for the midnight onslaught.

Boom! Boom!

The mortar fire continued all through the night with rhythmic and predictable frequency. Sometimes the earth shook. Sometimes I heard the crash and rattle of metal against metal somewhere in the unseen night. Sometimes the muffled sound came from farther away, with the only evidence being a momentary flash of bright, pervasive light on the horizon, a fleeting and unwelcome lapse from the darkness.

Night after night, often more than two to three nights

a week, we sat through the barrage with seldom a second thought.

It became a sort of background music to our sleepless nights — a mindless, aimless symphony conducted somewhere in the desperate folds of surrounding darkness, providing us with nothing more than a forgettable note and a fainting goodbye come morning.

As I lay there one night, simultaneously listening to and ignoring the bombardment, I thought to myself, *Well, if nothing else, the producers behind* Call of Duty *certainly pegged the sound spot on. Those video game mortar shells sound just like the real deal.*

My bunkmate, presumably sensing that I took notice of the latest round of mortar rounds, leaned over and joked, "Hey, those guys shooting at us, they're amateurs. All they've done is stuff a bunch of shrapnel into small tubes with barely enough explosives to pack any serious kind of punch."

He rolled back away from me as he closed his statement.

"If you can hear 'em, you're safe."

If I can hear 'em, I'm safe, I reassured myself.

One evening the sounds crept closer and closer to our station. Before I knew it, a *boom* unlike any I had ever heard before came crashing into me. The blast rocketed me backward before complete darkness closed in.

Shortly thereafter, I awoke. My friends stood around me, confirming that no real damage had been done, that the blast simply knocked me unconscious.

Frightened, yet relieved, I joked with myself once more, *If you can hear 'em, you're safe.*

And so our life at war continued. Day in and day out, often working 12 to 14 hours a day, outpacing the sun in all of its brilliant and fiery glory. Long before the sun awoke for the day, and long after it settled back down to sleep in the evening, we sat out there, sweating away our lives in that exploding inferno.

I didn't mind the long hours or the exhausting labor. It kept my mind off home, off my wife and girl, off myself. The hardest days were my days off.

I wonder what Paige's doing right now. I tormented myself, lying on my bunk midday.

I wonder what she's learning today or what she's even capable of by now. I wonder if she says "Mama" or if she understands what "Dada" means.

I realized I was missing her first Thanksgiving, her first Christmas and first New Year's — missing her first everything. It stung and bit and clawed at me. Those thoughts harassed me even more than the heat, or the darkness, or the *booms*, or the exhaustion I fought every single day.

While the tangible war raged all around me, the inner war of missing her, missing them — my daughter and my wife — brought me to my knees in agony and despair.

Days like this are going to kill me, I warned myself at last. *I can't just sit here thinking about Ava and Paige. I've got to keep my mind occupied with something.*

I knew of a nearby hospital that served both civilians

and military men alike and convinced myself that they needed help in one way or another.

Turned out I was right — they desperately needed help. However, being an aircraft mechanic, I had absolutely zero background in the medical field, which severely limited me in the tasks I could perform. They therefore assigned me to be a "body runner," which meant I transported patients from the ambulance or landing pad into the emergency room.

This, surprisingly, brought my first real taste of war.

I sat in that loading area, struggling between the thoughts of my wife and daughter and those of the gruesome scenes unfolding all around me. A call came in, and suddenly I rose to my feet, rushing to the back door to carry in the latest victim.

I carried civilians, innocent men, women and children, with their bodies torn to pieces. Soldiers soaked in blood and screaming in agony at the loss of a limb. Their faces were painted with fear and anguish. Even the scent hung morbidly in the air — a musty, miserable odor of death and decay. It was nearly more than I could handle and far more than I expected.

Each time I picked up one of those mangled masses of twisted and mutilated human proportions, I thought, *This could have been me. This seriously could be me, any time, any day. How can something like this happen? Why are these things allowed to happen to these people? How can life be so fragile?*

I took a step back and drew upon my childhood faith.

Seeing firsthand what the fragility and temporality of human life could amount to, I immediately called upon those teachings about God and his protection and provision that I had learned as a child. My desperate pleadings and petitions finally found their direction.

As I left the hospital that day, I prayed for the first time in a long while.

God, I still don't understand the things I see before me. I don't understand why I have been ripped away from my wife and 5-month-old daughter. I don't understand how men are capable of committing such unspeakable atrocities against one another. I don't understand why this darkness is allowed to survive and why you've brought me here into the very middle of it. But I do know, in some way, that you are in control over this and that I can trust in you to protect me and lead me through this darkness. God, please help me through this. Please keep me safe. Please bring me home to Ava and Paige.

Later that week I found a small church that met on base, and I grew comfortable meeting with them as often as I could. I prayed nearly every night through the rest of that war, forming a duet of sorts with the mortar rounds that blazed and burned all around.

Get me back home, I'd simply request. *Get me back to them. Get me back safe. Get me back soon.*

And God did. Nearly six months after I arrived in Afghanistan, my first deployment came to a close, and I received a one-way ticket back home.

I could afford only a simple *thank you.*

I officially returned home in February of 2010. I burst out of the plane to find my beautiful wife and my daughter, already nearly a year old, waiting for me by the baggage claim dock. I sped toward them with untold excitement and relief. All of the pain and turmoil I'd witnessed immediately melted away under the warmth of our reunion and newfound feelings of joy and fulfillment.

I snatched Paige in my arms and spun her around in pure delight. Her golden curls bounced excitedly around her smile, and she giggled with the anticipation of a child on Christmas morning. Ava joined the embrace, and my life felt full once again.

And yet, the joy and completion that came flooding back seemed to rush away just as quickly.

I expected to struggle upon arriving in Afghanistan, but I was not prepared for the struggle that ensued with my return home.

I continually felt uneasy, always fighting the feeling that something, or someone, was out to get me and my family.

Nothing is safe, my inner self, still emotionally deployed, would persist.

Everything is fine, my calm and rational self would contend.

But the never-ending battle continued. A back-and-forth tug-of-war between the mind and the heart. It was draining, exhausting, disruptive.

That hospital loading area haunted me day and night. The images continued to flood my mind. The smells and sounds followed me as my own shadow. The nightmares came at night, nearly every night, and Ava saw it all. She could feel the uneasiness and tension clinging to me, like humid summer air in the South.

At first she tried to understand. Her concern was evident, genuine and true.

But I couldn't express myself accurately. I couldn't help her to understand my struggles, and she slowly slipped away from trying to understand it herself.

I've got to get a handle on this, I thought. *I've got to seek out therapy or some sort of counseling to get me through.*

And so I did.

I contacted the military counseling center on base and scheduled my first appointment. It worked, but only for a time.

After several rounds of counseling, I sat across the table from my latest therapist, in awkward and unforced silence.

"Why are you having trouble opening up?" he inquired, glancing over the frames of his low-hanging glasses.

"It's nothing personal," I assured him. "It's just, I've been through this routine before, and I don't see that this time will be any different."

"How do you mean?" he prodded.

"It's like this. Step one: meet counselor. Step two: get to know counselor closely enough to gain confidence and comfort in opening up about my struggles and concerns.

Step three: make minimal progress as we dig deeper. Step four: counselor is deployed and relocated. Step five: repeat."

He remained silent.

"It's a miserable routine to develop, and I seem to be repeating it time and time again. I'm sick of regurgitating my story, my feelings, my worries and concerns and struggles. I'm sick of starting over just to start over."

Our meetings carried on in much the same fashion until he, too, was deployed, and I was reassigned to yet another counselor.

Not experiencing the growth and peace I craved, I turned to God for further guidance and support. He knew me completely, I figured, and he already understood where I came from and where I hoped to go. He comforted me on that battlefield, in that hospital and in those restless nights and stressful days back home. The same Jesus who suffered and died on my behalf thousands of years before still stood by my side in my time of suffering and my experience with death.

Paige and I attended church together regularly. I hoped that she would find the same guidance and peace that I found. She was a daddy's girl through and through. I'd bring her on walks with me, or on my errands, or even to work if I happened to be in charge of the shift that day.

"Hey, James! I see you brought your sidekick into work again," my co-workers joked.

"You know, Paige," they said, leaning in closely as if to reveal a secret, "your old man's not too good at ringing our sirens on the crash car. Do you think you could help him out?"

With an enthusiastic nod and joyful shout, she demanded to be lifted onto my shoulders to show Daddy how he was *supposed* to run the siren.

"Hey, that's pretty good!" I encouraged. "Now how about trying the loud speaker, too?"

She took control of the speaker and had the time of her life, throwing her head back and laughing at each unintelligible announcement.

⮘⮘⮘

"Hey, babe, Paige and I would love it if you joined us for church this Sunday. How about it?" I boldly asked over dinner one night.

"Mmm, I work this weekend, remember?" she answered absentmindedly.

"Well, maybe next Sunday, then?"

"Definitely! We can definitely see."

Each next Sunday would come and go, only to be met with a rotating lineup of "I'm too tired," or "I need to run errands," or "I'm visiting family and friends out of town." Always next Sunday, always excuses.

So, Paige and I continued to attend church together, and as she got older and understood more of what church was about, she asked if she could pray with me. It quickly became our regular daddy-daughter time — church on Sundays and prayer throughout the week. For some reason it gave me strength, kneeling by my daughter's bedside each night, hands clasped together, eyes closed, and praying to the God who I had lost as a child and found again in that battle-scarred hospital in Afghanistan.

Aside from the time spent with Paige and my time at church on Sunday morning, I pretty well kept to myself most days. I found comfort and rest and peace by myself, not having to explain my feelings or confusions, not having to communicate the struggles within me to someone who couldn't possibly understand. I found companionship in my growing relationship with God, but all the while, I pulled away from those around me.

"Ava, why won't you come to counseling with me, or church, or anything?" I begged one night, grasping at any hope that she might actually commit to coming. "I'm really trying to grow through all of this as best I can, and I want you there with me."

Never an answer. She offered only outright denials or flakey promises that never fulfilled themselves.

My wife had long since given up on trying to understand or support me through my struggles. I had long since given up on turning to her for those very same things. Even though my faith continued to grow, I often felt terribly and miserably alone.

I devoted myself to my career, and it kept me occupied most of the time. Working, studying, learning, growing, impressing, achieving — it all paid off. The Air Force promoted me to an E-5 Staff Sergeant, and I inherited increasingly time-consuming responsibilities. Soon they scheduled me to work almost every Sunday, and I found myself falling back out of church. I tried to attend Wednesday night services whenever possible, but my faith gradually weakened.

And then came the second deployment letter in May of 2012, this time to Africa.

My first deployment brought enough hardships, the effects seemed irreversible and I simply couldn't fathom the toll this second deployment would take on me and my family.

She's nearly 3 years old now, I worried. *She can think and feel and question and cry and wonder. The first time around only Ava and I felt and understood the separation, but now she will feel it, too.* That single thought stuck with me on the entire ride out. *She will feel it this time.*

I'm not sure which hit me harder when I first stepped off that plane in Djibouti — the sweltering African heat that seemingly boiled the very air in my lungs or the reality that 8,000 miles separated me from my wife and daughter for an undetermined length of time.

After a miserable and sleepless first night, day two finally came. I woke up and breathed for the first time in what seemed like weeks.

Last night was quiet and still. No mortars. No blasts.

It was my first realization that life in Djibouti would be drastically different than my time in Afghanistan. I was not immersed in combat this time and made sure to avoid hospitals at all costs.

Instead, I preoccupied myself by keeping in touch with

Ava and Paige as often as possible. Things progressed smoothly until about one month after I arrived, when I lost all contact with Ava.

I'd call. Straight to voicemail, no return call.

I'd email. No reply.

I'd try to Skype or FaceTime. No answer.

I'd write letters. No response.

Several torturous weeks dragged by like nails on a never-ending chalkboard.

Why am I not getting through? Why is she not answering? What could possibly be going on?

Time crept on without purpose or direction.

Finally, several weeks later, after frantically trying to reach her through every avenue possible, I got a hold of Ava for a brief moment while she was at work. Her opening line crushed me with the fullest force of destruction imaginable.

"I can't do this anymore, James," she stated. "I'm done."

I sat in stunned silence and disbelief.

"I can't handle this anymore. I'm so sorry!" she offered emptily.

"Babe, I know this has been tough. Believe me, I understand full well how difficult this has been, but please, PLEASE, don't do anything drastic."

Silence.

"Seriously, Ava, don't make any rash decisions. Please don't do anything that can't be undone. Just hang in there, and we'll talk about this when I get back."

"I'm just done, James. I'm done," she repeated, ignoring my pleas.

She hurried me off the phone and promised we'd talk again soon. "Soon" took a lot longer to arrive than I expected, and when it did, I had one simple request.

"Ava, let me speak to Paige. I want to talk to my little girl."

"Oh, she's busy right now. She's playing outside with friends, but maybe next time."

"Next time" took a lot longer to arrive than I expected, and when it did, I held fast to my one request.

"Ava, seriously, please let me talk to Paige. I miss my daughter, and I desperately want to hear her voice."

More excuses. More denials.

This carried on for weeks. Sporadic and infrequent phone conversations without ever speaking to Paige. Finally Ava budged and let me talk to my daughter, but it turns out that a 3-year-old quickly loses the focus and desire to carry on a telephone conversation with someone she can't see or touch.

"Hi, Daddy!" Her voice erupted through my headset.

"Paige! Hey, baby! How are you? How have you been? Do you miss Daddy?"

"Yeah! I love you, Daddy!"

"I love you, too, baby! Are you having fun?"

"Yeah, Daddy! I love you!"

She said nothing else.

"Ava, would you let me video chat with Paige? I'm dying to see her and interact with her."

"She ran off again. Maybe next time, though."

And the cycle started all over again.

For the next five months, I barely spoke to my daughter, maybe once every other week, and only for minutes at a time. Very rarely would Ava set up a video call between Paige and me, and even that lasted shorter than our phone conversations.

I implored Ava for answers. Answers for everything. How she was doing. How she felt. Why she felt the need to give up. Why she limited my communication with Paige. No answers. No clarity. No peace.

Again, the questions and doubts and frustrations swelled within me. *How can this possibly be happening right now? God, why are you letting this happen? What went wrong? Why do I deserve this?*

No answers. No clarity. No peace.

The months dragged on in much the same fashion. Little to no communication with Ava or Paige, little to no understanding and guidance from God.

My friends sensed my turmoil and kept me occupied with any activity they could find. We'd travel as far as we were able. We'd explore the local hiking trails and tourist destinations, diving, swimming, discovering — always moving.

I turned my focus back to work, trying to distract myself from sorrow and loneliness in those 14-hour days. I even volunteered at a local wildlife refuge and orphanage.

There was a young girl who reminded me a lot of

Paige. Her father worked at the orphanage, and she spent most of her days there while she played with the other children. She was free-spirited and loved to dance and sing. She burst at the seams with joyful excitement whenever I entered the room.

I showed up one Tuesday to start my routine work, but the young girl was missing. I spotted her father across the room and walked over to him. Despite my time there, the language barrier remained strong and several layers thick. However, we were able to piece together minimal conversations.

"Where is she, your daughter?" I dropped my hand to my waist, palm-down, to emphasize the reference. "She's not here?" I looked around, confused.

"Oh," he replied lethargically. "Yes, she died last night." He walked away without so much as a tear in his eye or a tremble in his voice.

How can that be it? I struggled. *How can that be his reaction? My daughter is alive and well, and it tears me to pieces that I am not able to speak to her, to hold her, to run and dance and play with her every day. His daughter has died, never to grace his presence again, and THAT is how he responds?*

I could not handle it. A grown man, volunteering my time in a ramshackle orphanage, amidst a hopeless and death-riddled culture, I broke down and collapsed in tears in front of the very children I hoped to encourage and support.

"I'm sorry, but this obviously isn't going to work

anymore," I admitted, turning to the closest worker. "I can't do this."

And I left.

I saw my fair share of death in Djibouti, just as I had in Afghanistan. While making our rounds in local villages, we stumbled upon the gruesome remains of human bodies that had been stuffed inside large rubber tires and lit on fire.

I had twice been mere feet away from catastrophic collisions between fully armed fighter jets loaded with active missiles and wayward 747s coming in for emergency landings.

I saw the loss of innocent life after an airstrike proved to be inaccurate due to faulty intelligence. Innocent women and children died from a regrettable error.

I saw vicious wildlife, including cheetahs and baboons, ruthlessly attack without apparent rhyme or reason.

And once, while hiking the volcanic rim at Lake Assal and admiring the breathtakingly beautiful crystal-clear pools below, I lost my footing and slid 20 feet down the side of a steep canyon, slicing my hand and rendering myself bruised, broken and deserted with no way out. Several hours passed by with no relief. A simple prayer escaped my lips.

God, please get me out. It can't end like this. Not here. Not now. Please, get me out. Keep me safe.

And he did. He answered me and provided yet again. In a land dominated by death, he provided and sustained my life.

After that afternoon in the orphanage, I met with our chaplain regularly. I knew that with everything before me, the death, the hopelessness, the loneliness, the struggle back home and the separation, I would need something to lean on. I knew it could not be me. I knew it had to be Jesus. I believed he already suffered in my place so that I could find peace in him while I struggled through my own suffering. I had to trust in him.

I still could not understand why things were allowed to happen the way they did, but I grew more and more comfortable knowing that God would lead me according to his purpose and that as I entrusted more of my life to him, I would find greater peace in not depending on myself or my own understanding.

I continued to pray every single night. I prayed that I would return home safe. That Ava and I would be able to talk through our issues and that I would be able to see Paige.

Ava had cut ties with all of our mutual friends and many family members, so getting in touch with her proved to be nearly impossible. However, upon receiving my orders to return home, I connected with a close friend who still kept in touch with her. He picked Paige up from Ava's in order to meet me at the airport upon my return flight home.

Two words permeated my very being on the entire flight: *See Paige.*

See Paige.

In just a few hours you will get to see Paige again! I

reassured myself constantly. *You'll get to hold her and talk to her and listen to her and see how smart and strong and beautiful she's become.*

See Paige.

I landed sometime between 6 and 7 a.m. Compared to the blistering 140-degree heat in Djibouti, the chilly December air in North Carolina invigorated and refreshed me.

I exited the plane, hustled down the various corridors leading to the waiting platform and rounded the final corner to baggage claim.

There she slouched, tired, cold and barely able to stay awake. Her beautiful blond hair, now longer than I'd ever seen before, lazily drooped over her eyes, highlighting her exhaustion. She wore dark leggings tucked into sparkly silver boots, with a warm jacket buttoned nearly all the way up.

"Well, aren't you the most adorable bundle of warmth I've ever seen!" I shouted as I ran up to her.

"Daddy!" she screamed in return, with excitement glowing from every inch of her miniature frame.

The sun had just risen over the horizon, and as I lifted her in my arms, she smiled and laughed and continually grabbed and pinched my cheeks to "make sure that Daddy is real!"

We climbed into my friend's car to head home, and she grabbed my arm and demanded, "No, Daddy! You sit in back with me!"

Life felt complete once more. In that moment, the

death and decay I left behind and the domestic turbulence I had yet to encounter both ceased to exist entirely. That moment was perfection. Paige and I together at last. Daddy and daughter reunited.

Three full days passed before Ava contacted me, asking to meet up and talk things through.

As she pulled up in her car, I grew nervous and anxious. We were about to confront months of silence and confusion.

However, whatever conversation I had hoped to have with Ava, our first meeting did not go as expected.

I anticipated some sort of apology for the things she had done, for the way she had acted, for keeping Paige away from me for so long. At the very least I assumed she'd offer an explanation. Nothing of the sort came out.

Instead, Ava began with, "I don't think Paige should stay with you right now. You are incredibly stressed out, and I simply can't trust you with her yet."

Her statement sounded cold, callous and calculated. Anger engulfed me and seemed to pulse through me like the blood in my veins. Frustration dripped out of every pore. My entire body screamed out in bewilderment.

"You can't trust me?" I shot back heatedly.

"I'm not the one who ran off with Paige while you were deployed. I'm not the one who stole her from your life and limited your interaction with her. I'm not the one who gave up on this family without any warning, or concern, or explanation. I'm the one who can be trusted!"

She remained unfazed.

"Listen," I continued. "I know that we had a rough patch when I came back last time, but that's exactly why I wanted you to join me in counseling. We can work this out if we work together."

Her expression changed not a bit. Her demeanor held fast.

"Marriage is important to me, Ava. *This* is important to me. Me, you, Paige. Our family is important to me. This isn't something I can just walk away from."

The argument twisted back and forth. Neither of us giving an inch, neither of us gaining ground. She was resolved to file for divorce and fight for custody over Paige. She had kept silently isolated for so long that my words were having, and could have, very little impact on her decision.

I begged and pleaded to seek reconciliation together, to piece back together this broken shadow of a marriage we once had. She stood staunchly opposed. In her mind, it was over.

In our earlier years, Ava and I had become close friends with another couple named David and Lisa. They were extremely supportive of me in my time overseas and in the difficult transition period upon my first return. I had been staying with them since I got home from Djibouti, at least until Ava and I sorted things out. But as I watched her leave with Paige that day, I knew I needed a change of scenery. David agreed to drop me off at my house, and within minutes, we were silently on our way.

As I stepped out of his car and onto that lonely stretch

of driveway that once led home, I turned to David and offered a miserable, "Thanks."

"If you need anything at all, James, please don't hesitate to call. We are here for you, you know that, right?"

I nodded.

He drove away.

My home turned out to be even emptier than I felt inside. When Ava left it, she sold nearly all of my possessions, canceled my credit cards and moved in with a man whom she had been seeing during my absence. My cell phone, computer, clothes, furniture, gadgets, gizmos and truck were gone. All that remained was my bed, a couch and the television set. She even cleared out our joint bank account. I quite literally had nothing but the skeletal frame of our house and the emptiness that festered within.

The months that followed brought all of my deepest fears and concerns to center stage. Despite having survived two deployments, one in the heart of war, I was not prepared for the battle that ensued.

Our divorce papers were processing and were set to clear that summer. Meanwhile, my wife had raged an all-out assault on the issue of custody over Paige.

As the custody war raged on, I sat in an awfully tidy and organized office, trying not to lose all sense of control at the words I read.

"Alcoholic, verbally abusive, physically threatening," I read aloud, equally to myself as to my lawyer. "Neglectful to Paige."

I looked at my lawyer. "She even claims that I'm the one who had an affair! Can you believe this?"

He walked around the desk and stood behind me as I raked through lie after lie after lie.

"She's just trying to play all of her cards before you have a chance to play any of yours. All we can do is make the truth known and prove that these accusations aren't substantial."

"I trusted this woman, you know? We've been married for five and a half years — I never could have imagined her doing this."

My words offered no relief. My lawyer's words offered no relief. Just as in that Afghani hospital room, I realized relief could come from only one place. So I redirected my words yet again, in utter frustration.

God, how can this be possible? Why are you allowing this to happen? After all you've put me through, after the challenges I've already faced and overcome, after all of the hurt and loneliness, how could you possibly be watching over this for good? Are you even watching over this? Why must I always be challenged? Haven't I been challenged enough?

I began to doubt God again and decided to pursue resolution through my own efforts. I left the military on a generous retirement package and put every last dime into the legal battle for Paige.

The divorce papers were finalized in June of 2013. The woman I once loved and trusted and treasured was, officially, no longer a part of my life.

I saw Paige from time to time, on the rare occasions when Ava would allow me to contact them and arrange a meeting. I spent most of my days painfully and irreconcilably heartbroken.

తతత

Then in December of that same year, the verdict came in. The final blow. The judge rose and fixed his eyes upon me.

"Your daughter will come and stay with you during the summer, spring and Christmas holiday seasons," he stated plainly, as if rattling off the upcoming weather forecast to a disinterested audience over his morning newspaper.

"Other than that," he continued, "she shall remain under the care and supervision of her mother, at her residence in North Carolina."

The decision devastated me. For a man who'd seen death and destruction beyond measure, this two-sentence assault proved to be the fatal blow.

So this is it. Three times a year she's mine. Only three times a year. God, how did it come to this? Can't you change this? Why won't you change this? Please change this.

The doubt lingered, the understanding continued to evade me. The frustration and confusion rose to all-time highs.

I took a brief inventory of my life at that point. My

career was over, my marriage as well. My daughter, fractionally mine. Nothing remained for me in North Carolina except heartache and pain, so I decided to move back home to Michigan in an effort to start fresh and sort things out.

And that's when I found hope.

∞∞∞

I first met Sophie through a friend of a friend and quickly noticed her vibrant, upbeat and positive attitude. She reminded me a lot of Paige, filled with love, joy and encouragement, except that she had substantial, uplifting and meaningful wisdom and advice to offer.

"Hey, James, how would you like to join me for church this Sunday, at New Hope Community Church, right here in Charlotte?"

Despite my struggles with God, I ached to get back to church, to get back in relationship with him, so I jumped at the opportunity.

"Absolutely! I would love to!"

Weeks went by, and every Sunday I found myself happily attending church services with Sophie by my side. I shared my entire story with her, and she listened patiently, gently and supportively. Others in the church introduced themselves as well and connected with me through similar struggles. I felt all of the burdens and pain I had been carrying throughout the years slowly and steadily lift off my shoulders. I no longer found peace in being alone but rather in confiding my struggles and frustrations in these men and women who genuinely cared for me.

A few months passed, and Sophie sat me down after the service one Sunday.

"James, I've noticed a huge difference in you. You know that?" She didn't wait for a reply.

"I'm amazed at how far you've come, given the struggles in your life and all you've been through. It's truly incredible."

I paused for just a moment, reflecting on the journey that God had brought me through.

"You know, Sophie," I began. "I had my ups and downs with God throughout those hardships. The terrible things I witnessed, the awful divorce with Ava, losing Paige. My faith was definitely tested. But the people here at New Hope Community Church have helped me to see the beauty in my storm. My suffering isn't unique. Jesus suffered far worse than I have, and God purposed that suffering for his ultimate good. I still don't understand my suffering all the time, but I have full confidence that God is working all things together for my good, to strengthen me and draw me closer to him. I used to look at my struggles and see doubt and frustration. Now I can look at my struggles and see Jesus. Nothing provides me more hope or understanding than that."

With one hand she grabbed my arm and pulled it tightly against hers. With her other hand she shaded her eyes from the sun and squinted up into the bright summer air.

"I'm glad to hear it, James," she said, grinning.

A smile crept across my face as my gaze joined hers in the sky. The future was wide open. I felt complete again, more complete than I had felt in a long, long time.

CONCLUSION

Every story in this book shares at least two things in common: Hope destroyed, and a new hope discovered. First, each person tells about the events or circumstances that left him or her devastated. But then each person also tells how and where he or she found strength and healing and a fresh start in life.

This book and its stories represent the real-life experiences of some of the people who attend New Hope Community Church. Real people with real problems who found the strength and the source for hope when all seemed lost. And who wish to share that hope with you.

Many whose lives dramatically turn around cite two verses from the Bible as being especially reassuring. The first one reads, "For I know the thoughts that I think toward you, says the LORD, thoughts of peace and not of evil, to give you a future and a hope" (Jeremiah 29:11).

This means that God has a plan and a purpose for our lives. The thoughts and plan that God has for me and you are to bring us peace and not evil. God has a plan that will give people a future and a hope. The trouble is that wrong choices made by others or by ourselves cause all kinds of problems. Problems like in the stories you just read.

We all miss the mark in regard to living according to God's plan. The Bible calls this sin, and as you just read in these stories, sin destroys God's plan for our lives. But there is hope! God loves each of us and wants to restore all that sin destroys. We believe this book is just one way God can reach you with the truth that God still has thoughts to bring you a future and a hope.

No matter who you are, we believe that God loves you and came to save you. God came so that the pain, the despair, the emptiness can be replaced with a joy and a peace that comes from putting your faith in Jesus Christ.

The second verse people often find reassuring and encouraging reads, "But Jesus looked at them and said to them, 'With men this is impossible, but with God all things are possible'" (Matthew 19:26).

The people who share their stories in this book are just like you and me. They found themselves in situations that seemed impossible to change. *Would they ever have a hope or a future?* But with God, all things are possible. No matter how far from God they strayed. No matter how far from God *you* may have strayed. No matter how sinful your life may be, with God there is hope.

I would like to invite you to come and visit with us here at New Hope Community Church and discover for yourself the same strength and source that has changed the lives of so many. This hope for something better, something life changing, is found by accepting Jesus Christ as Lord and Savior.

You may have never asked Jesus to come into your life, or you may have felt close to him before but know you are not currently where you should be. Why not pray right now, and start discovering God's plan and purpose for your life?

Lord, I need your help. After reading these stories, I realize that what is missing in my life is you. My life has been filled with pain, guilt, disappointment and shame. I know that right now my life is separated from you, but I want that to change. I am sorry for the choices I've made that ended up hurting myself or others and that denied you. I do believe that you have been reaching out to me, and now I am reaching out to you. I am asking you, Lord, to come into my life. Come and begin the healing that is needed deep inside. Come and fill my life with your spirit, and lead me to what is true and right. I commit my life to you. Amen.

The stories of transformed lives because of God's love are still being written right here in Charlotte. Find out what might be ahead in your story with Jesus Christ as your Savior. I hope to see you Sunday!

Pastor Randy Royston
New Hope Community Church
Charlotte, Michigan

We would love for you to join us at
New Hope Community Church!

We meet Sundays 10:30 a.m. and 6 p.m.
and Wednesdays at 7 p.m.

Our address is
436 W Harris Street, Charlotte, MI 48813

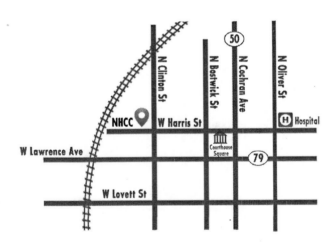

Please call us at 517.543.8603 for directions,
or contact us at www.charlottenewhopechurch.com.